Workplace Sexual Harassment

ANNE LEVY
Michigan State University

MICHELE PALUDI
*Paludi & Associates,
Consultants in Sexual Harassment*

Prentice Hall, Upper Saddle River, NJ 07458

Sr. Acquisitions Editor: Donald J. Hull
Editorial Assistant: Jim Campbell
Editor-in-Chief: James Boyd
Director of Development: Steve Deitmer
Production Editor: David G. Cotugno
Managing Editor: Valerie Q. Lentz
Manufacturing Buyer: Ken Clinton
Assistant Editor: John Larkin
Cover Design: Bruce Kenselaar
Cover Photo Research: Karen Branson
Cover Art/Photo: Kiwi Design
Interior Design: Ann France

Copyright © 1997 by Prentice-Hall, Inc.
A Simon & Schuster Company
Upper Saddle River, New Jersey 07458

Library of Congress Cataloging-in-Publication Data

Levy, Anne, 1950–
    Workplace sexual harassment / Anne Levy, Michele Paludi.
      p.   cm.
    Includes bibliographical references and index.
    ISBN 0-13-450560-3 (pbk.)
      1. Sexual harassment—United States.   2. Sex discrimination in
    employment—United States.   3. Sex role in the work environment—
    United States.   4. Sexual harassment—Law and legislation—United
    States.   I. Paludi, Michele Antoinette.   II. Title.
    HD6060.3.L486   1996
    331.13'3'0973—dc20   96-22254
                                                                      CIP

Prentice-Hall International (UK) Limited, London
Prentice-Hall of Australia Pty. Limited, Sydney
Prentice-Hall Canada, Inc., Toronto
Prentice-Hall Hispanoamericana, S.A., Mexico
Prentice-Hall of India Private Limited, New Delhi
Prentice-Hall of Japan, Inc., Tokyo
Simon & Schuster Asia Pte. Ltd., Singapore
Editora Prentice-Hall do Brasil, Ltda., Rio de Janeiro

Printed in the United States of America
10 9 8 7 6 5 4 3 2

For George and Elaine Cattermole
Anne Levy

For Sophie and Sam Picciocca
Michele Paludi

Contents

Preface

In the fall of 1991, we, like most of the nation, were riveted to our television sets watching the Senate Judiciary Committee's hearings on the confirmation of Clarence Thomas for a position on the United States Supreme Court. We listened to Professor Anita Hill describe her experiences with her former boss, then the head of the Equal Employment Opportunity Commission, the agency responsible for enforcing sexual harassment policies and procedures. We remember Professor Hill describing her background as one of thirteen children born on a farm in Okmulgee County in Oklahoma and recall her introducing to the committee and to the world, her father, Albert, her mother, Erma, and her sisters. She was Anita Hill, the daughter and the sibling, but soon she would become Anita Hill, the symbol.

Professor Hill took on an almost mystical quality, representing for many women the struggle they had gone through to be accepted in the workplace. As she described Clarence Thomas's use of work situations to describe sex and sex acts he had observed, the nation gasped. She discussed her worry that if she spoke out against Chairperson Thomas's behavior, she would suffer retaliation, and women nodded in understanding. As she stated:

> I began to feel severe stress on the job. I began to be concerned that Clarence Thomas might take out his anger with me by degrading me or not giving me important assignments. I also thought that he might find an excuse for dismissing me. . . . I was handicapped because I feared that if he found out he might make it more difficult for me to find other employment, and I might be dismissed from the job I had.

We also listened and watched Judge Thomas deny her claims and label the hearings a "travesty," stating:

> I deny each and every allegation against me. . . . I think that this hearing should never occur in America. This is a case in which this sleaze, this dirt, was

searched for by staffers of members of this committee, was then leaked to the media, and this committee and body validated it and displayed it in prime time over our entire nation. . . . The Supreme Court is not worth it. No job is worth it. I think something is dreadfully wrong with this country, when any person, any person in this free country would be subjected to this.

Sometime during the three days of testimony by Professor Hill, Judge Thomas, and witnesses for both parties, we learned that Professor Hill had taken and passed a lie detector test. Nevertheless, we were told that dozens of public opinion polls showed that people believed Thomas by a margin of two to one, and we heard a variety of so-called motives for Professor Hill's allegations. Not the least of these were political aspirations or the revenge of a scorned lover.

In the days and months that followed the hearings, we noticed a change in the tenor of the country. Justice Thomas was confirmed, but only on a two-vote margin, the closest ever for a confirmed Justice, becoming Justice on a court that, ironically, has the responsibility to decide sexual harassment cases under federal law. Even now, however, there is a sense that the charges have not gone away. Professor Hill did not seek political office, people began to question the motives of some of the witnesses against her, and the two-to-one ratio of those who believed Clarence Thomas has reversed. Within two years of the Thomas hearings, more people stated that they believed Anita Hill rather than Justice Thomas.

It was amazing that the Senate never resolved anything concerning allegations of sexual harassment or anything else. According to some polls, many Americans believed Judge Thomas was acquitted of charges of sexual harassment. Not so! The committee was not charged with investigating or deciding the validity of Professor Hill's allegations, and it did not. Whether the members believed her or not, they still could confirm Judge Thomas. To this day, we are unsure what the three days of testimony really meant. We are sure, however, that they raised the consciousness of every employer, manager, and employee, and heralded an unprecedented national preoccupation with an area of the law.

When we met a few years later, we both talked about the hearings, our views about sexual harassment in general, and the issues raised by both Professor Hill and then-Judge Thomas, in particular. We found, despite the difference in our backgrounds and academic fields, that we shared concerns about how the Senate Judiciary Committee had done its job and how the nation had approached this sensitive area. We agreed that the questions that were asked by the senators were most inappropriate, raised without thought, planning, or understanding of this complex subject. We also feared that women and men who wanted to file charges of sexual harassment at their company might expect the investigation to be similar or identical to the Hill-Thomas hearings, despite the fact that such a procedure would undoubtedly violate the law.

What we realized most in our talks was that a lack of education and understanding was at the heart of most of the insensitivity. Recognizing that this lack of understanding could be corrected and that it made sense, fiscally and ethically, for business to handle sexual harassment situations appropriately, we decided to write this book.

We wanted to bring our respective disciplines together, as usually happens in a sexual harassment lawsuit, to educate about sexual harassment from two perspectives. Anne is an attorney and professor of business law; Michele is a research psychologist, trainer, and expert witness in cases involving sexual harassment. Together, we outline the legal and psychological issues involved in labeling and controlling workplace sexual harassment.

Although many businesspeople may believe that the legal issues are the only ones of importance in the area of sexual harassment, in actuality, they should be the least important consideration. Harassment of workers can indeed result in extensive legal liability, yet any businessperson or manager who allows a workplace environment to become so oppressive that it reaches the level of a legally defined "hostile environment" is not displaying good business sense. Not only is harassment potentially expensive in the legal arena, it exacts a tremendous cost in worker morale and potential.

The term *sexual harassment* can be confusing because it has both a legal and a logical definition. To be termed sexual harassment by the law, harassing conduct or behavior must reach a level that the courts have defined as "beyond trivial or merely offensive." Sexual harassment as a behavior term, however, is quite different. Situations in a workplace may well be termed sexual harassment yet not reach the level of legally defined sexual harassment. What must be made clear to all workers, however, is that harassment because of another's gender does not belong in the workplace, whether such behavior does or does not meet the legal standard.

Ignoring any situation that presents evidence of sexual harassment, whether it falls under the logical or the legal definition, is *legally* risky. Conduct that to some might seem trivial or merely offensive cannot be ignored in a workplace for several reasons. First, the courts continue to advance their views of what conduct is "permissible" and what is not. In addition, even if the law were not in as much flux as it is, it is always difficult to predict where the lines may be drawn in a courtroom. This is especially true if, as is now often the case, a jury is involved. Another reason to take all substantiated charges of offensive conduct very seriously and deal with them appropriately, as is only too clear to any manager, is that the reported behavior may be only the tip of a very precipitous iceberg. Additionally, there is no doubt that an accumulation of "merely offensive or trivial" behavior will soon result in a legal liability, which no business wants to deal with, for tangible economic reasons as well as for the more intangible, but just as detrimental, effects on the company's image and reputation. Lastly, the government agencies that are given the power to investigate and deal with such matters, as well as the courts, have made it very clear that they will be looking very carefully at how the company has dealt internally with any possible problems in order to determine liability.

Thus, although it is important to know what the law says about sexual harassment, one must always keep in mind that dealing with it adequately means handling situations long before they reach the level of creating legal liability. This requires a complete understanding of the psychology of sexual harassment: what it is, why and how it affects certain workers, and how to handle situations in an appropriate manner.

All managers, not just those designated as equal employment officers, bear a great responsibility for prohibiting sexual harassment in the workplace and especially for handling situations correctly when problems arise. As will later be seen, lawsuits against specific managers for not carrying out the dictates of equal employment law are possible, often because a supervisor, although not involved in the harassment, ignored the situation. Even without individual liability, however, the supervisor can cause extensive liability for his or her employer. In *Andrews v. City of Philadelphia*,[1] a case involving a "hostile work environment" in the city police department's Accident Investigation Division (AID), the court noted that the supervisor's responsibility is high:

> Where, as here, the employer's supervisory personnel manifested unmistakeable acquiescence in or approval of the harassment, the burden on the employer seeking to avoid liability is especially high. The City must demonstrate that its supervisory employees investigated the plantiff's complaint and took appropriate action to curb sexism at AID.

This responsibility requires those in authority to make more than a determination of whether the company is legally liable when a report of harassing behavior is lodged or a situation observed. Certain behavior or conduct must be curtailed because of its negative effect on workers, whether or not it would, alone, form the basis for a lawsuit. Thus, in order to deal with such matters appropriately, a good understanding of the psychology of sexual harassment is, in many ways, far more vital than a comprehension of the legal standards.

Incidents of sexual harassment are best viewed as smoke that indicates that, although there is the potential for a legal bonfire, there is still time to prevent overwhelming damage. This metaphor is often used in the law, and as any lawyer can substantiate, it is much easier and less costly to remove flammable objects before a fire breaks out than it is to fight a raging fire. Once the problem has gotten out of control, there will be no recourse but to call in expensive experts to deal with the situation.

How expensive can ignoring the smoke be for a business? The answer is, as with all situations where law gets involved, very. Changes in the law in recent years are making it easier for victims to win cases and to receive high verdicts. Since 1991, for example, federal law allows recovery of both punitive and compensatory damages, a type of recovery that many state laws have allowed for several years. In many harassment cases, this type of damage award can be very large, and recent jury verdicts for successful plaintiffs have reached the $3.8 million mark. The law also allows recovery of attorney fees, back pay, and front pay, and courts are authorized to force, through injunctions, the reinstatement and promotion of victims, the award of seniority, and judge's supervision over the institution of policies and procedures that are legally satisfactory.

The increasing number of complaints filed each year shows that many businesses are not dealing with the problem effectively. Since 1990, the number of sexual harassment complaints filed with the Equal Employment Opportunity Commission has more than doubled to twelve thousand per year, and the EEOC is only one of several avenues that workers have for coming forward with charges.

Once charges are filed, it will be very difficult for a business to deal with the problem internally. Ironically, it is only at this point that an understanding of the legal perspective will be as important as the psychological. Unfortunately, at this point, it may help only in determining a settlement figure. Letting a situation get to that point is not just foolhardy, but a very inefficient and risky business practice. If a company needs to call a lawyer to defend a sexual harassment lawsuit, the company probably lost an earlier opportunity to deal with the situation in a proper and inexpensive manner. As is usual in this society, the law steps in when business doesn't "take care of business" in a way that the society demands. When the damage costs in sexual harassment cases are added to the expense in time and dollars of defending a lawsuit, it becomes clear that any company that finds itself named in a sustainable sexual harassment lawsuit has exercised very bad business judgment.

Thus, sexual harassment is a serious organizational problem. To date, there is no text that addresses the legal issues, incidence, psychological dimensions, and explanatory models of sexual harassment. This book fills a need in the literature on workplace sexual harassment. We focus on variables that can assist organizations in confronting and preventing sexual harassment, including manager training, education and awareness, and psychotherapeutic techniques for families and friends of sexually harassed individuals as well as the victims themselves.

We begin with a discussion of the legal issues involved in understanding why sexual harassment occurs in the workplace, including an overview of the American legal system. We then address sexual harassment from the psychological perspective, including individuals' attitudes about and attributions of sexual harassment, and how images that women and men workers have in their heads get transformed into discriminatory behavior in the workplace. These chapters constitute part I of this book.

Part II of this book centers around preventing sexual harassment through the establishment and enforcement of an effective policy statement prohibiting sexual harassment in the workplace and the enforcement of effective grievance procedures for investigating and resolving complaints of sexual harassment. We also discuss the Equal Employment Opportunity Commission's role in investigating complaints of sexual harassment should an individual file a complaint outside her or his company.

In the appendices, we offer several resources to help managers with their own training in sexual harassment, including the Equal Employment Opportunity Commission Policy Guidance, suggestions for interviewing complainants, and sample training programs.

We both believe that the best protection organizations can give employees lies in the power of understanding and education about sexual harassment. It is our hope that the managers and other concerned individuals who read this book can successfully impart this information to the individuals in their lives.

Notes

1. Andrews v. City of Philadelphia, 895 F.2d 1469, (3d Cir. 1990).

About the Authors

Anne Levy

Anne C. Levy, J.D., is an Associate Professor of Law, Public Policy and Business in the Eli Broad College of Business and Graduate School of Management at Michigan State University. She teaches courses in the legal environment of business for undergraduates and graduates in the MBA and Executive MBA programs. In addition, she teaches courses in law for MSU's Women's Studies Program.

Before joining the faculty at Michigan State University, Professor Levy served as Judicial Law Clerk to The Honorable Patricia J. Boyle, Associate Justice of the Michigan Supreme Court. Prior to attending law school, she spent many years in the field of public relations.

Professor Levy has published a variety of articles on the subject of the law of sexual harassment in publications such as the *Albany Law Review,* the *Kansas Law Review,* and the *St. Louis University Law Review.* In addition, she has been involved in sexual harassment seminars and training sessions for employees, managers, students, faculty, and administrators.

As a consultant, Professor Levy aids attorneys involved in sexual harassment cases in understanding the law and preparing evidence. She is also involved in the training and preparation of expert witnesses.

Michele Paludi

Michele A. Paludi, Ph.D., is an internationally recognized expert in academic and workplace sexual harassment. She is the editor of *Ivory Power: Sexual Harassment on Campus* (SUNY Press, 1990), coauthor of *Academic and*

Workplace Sexual Harassment: A Resource Manual (SUNY Press, 1991), and editor of *Sexual Harassment on College Campuses: Abusing the Ivory Power* (SUNY Press, 1996). Dr. Paludi is currently writing *Sexual Harassment of Adolescents by Teachers and Peers* for SUNY Press.

Dr. Paludi is principal of Michele Paludi & Associates, Consultants in Sexual Harassment, and offers education and training in issues related to sexual harassment at schools, colleges, and organizations. In addition, she is an expert witness for academic and court proceedings involving sexual harassment.

For her research, training, and investigative work, Dr. Paludi received the 1992 Progress in Equity Award from the National and New York State Chapter of the American Association of University Women. She is also the 1988 recipient of the Emerging Leader Award from the Committee on Women of the American Psychological Association. In 1992, the YWCA awarded Dr. Paludi their Woman of Vision Award for Advocacy. Dr. Paludi was named the 1994 Woman of the Year by the New York State Business and Professional Women's Organization.

Dr. Paludi's book, *Ivory Power,* was named the 1992 recipient of the Gustavus Myers Center Award for the Outstanding Book on Human Rights in the United States.

Dr. Paludi is the author of nine books on sexual harassment, the psychology of women, and gender. Her coedited book, *Psychology of Women: Handbook of Issues and Theories* was recently named the outstanding academic book in the United States by the American Library Association.

She has held faculty positions at Franklin and Marshall College, Kent State University, Hunter College, and Union College.

Dr. Paludi was a member of Governor Cuomo's Task Force on Sexual Harassment.

Acknowledgments

We would like to thank the following family members, friends, and colleagues for their encouragement and support during the research and writing of our book:

Nancy Adamson
Lorraine Hollar
Allan Levy
Elvin Lashbrook, Jr.
—Anne Levy

Rosalie Paludi
Lucille Paludi
Fr. John Provost
James Tedisco
Mary Macherone
Charles Macherone
Ginny Campbell
Rev. Richard Campbell
—Michele Paludi

PART

Understanding Sexual Harassment

Legal and Psychological Perspectives

CHAPTER 1

The American Legal System

We are looking at a charge that is ten years old. It wasn't done yesterday, it wasn't done last week. That is some twenty times beyond the statute of limitations. The statute of limitations, as I understand it, is a number of days, or in some events as long as six months. This is twenty times the statute of limitations. Basically, what we are called upon to prove or you are called upon to prove is a negative. You are called upon to prove that ten years ago you didn't do something. I am not sure how you do that. I am not sure how you prove a negative.

—Senator Brown,
Senate Judiciary Confirmation Hearings
of Clarence Thomas, 1991

CASE STUDY

Fred Farnsworth is very upset. He has just received a phone call from his lawyer, who told Fred that he is being sued by a former employee for sexual harassment. The lawyer told Fred that he faces various statutory, as well as some common-law, claims and that they need to talk soon. Fred is upset not only because he doesn't like the idea that he is being sued but also because he didn't understand anything that his lawyer said to him. "I'm being told that a 'girlie calendar' and 'girlie magazines' in the lounge areas may have violated the federal law, even though a recently passed state law

---

specifically protects such displays. Also, I'm being told that the employee is claiming that one of my supervisors intentionally inflicted emotional distress. What the heck does all that mean? How do I know what type of behavior will result in emotional distress? Will I be facing several different lawsuits in several different courts?"

Introduction

In order to better understand the law of sexual harassment, you need to have a basic understanding of the legal process at work in the United States. Various courts and government institutions are involved in carrying out this country's laws and have a continuing effect on the development of sexual harassment law.

The Court Systems

There are two parallel court systems in the United States: the federal system and the state systems. The jurisdiction of each system is specified by statute or in the federal or state constitutions. Generally, the federal courts hear cases involving laws that are passed by Congress, questions concerning the federal Constitution, and civil disputes between residents of two different states (called *diversity jurisdiction*). State courts adjudicate matters that concern laws passed by that state's legislature, the state's constitution, and civil disputes between people who are both classified as being residents of that state. Occasionally, federal courts may hear state-law claims when a case involves both federal and state matters, but the federal court must adhere to the state court's precedents in making those decisions.

> *Thus, Fred's concern in the case study that he may be forced into several lawsuits in several different courts is probably unfounded. The federal court could decide all of the claims, even though some may be based on state law.*

In the federal system, generally speaking, the federal district court is the lowest-level court. Federal district courts are usually classified as the "trial courts," meaning that they will be the first courts to hear cases, listen to the evidence, and make decisions about disputed facts about the applicable law. These decisions may be made by a judge or a jury, depending on whether a jury trial is allowed and on the preference of the parties. A jury trial must be made available when the Seventh Amendment to the Constitution requires it or when Congress specifies it in a federal law. Since 1991, federal law has allowed for a jury in employment discrimination lawsuits, including sexual harassment claims.

Once a decision has been given in the federal district court, the parties will have an opportunity to appeal the decision to the circuit courts of appeals. There are thirteen circuit courts of appeals, which are responsible for hearing appeals from federal district courts in a designated region. After a decision has been reached in a circuit court of appeal, either party may apply to the United States Supreme Court for leave to appeal. If the Supreme Court decides to hear a case, it will grant *certiorari,* which means that the case will be argued before the highest court. The United States Supreme Court usually gets involved only in cases that present issues of vital importance or that will allow the Court to settle a disagreement in decisions between the circuits (i.e., the courts of appeals are coming to opposite conclusions about the same issue). There are currently several such situations in the area of sexual harassment, but the Supreme Court has not chosen to accept cases that would allow it to settle the issues, uniformly denying *certiorari.* When *certiorari* is denied, it does not necessarily mean that the Supreme Court agrees with the lower court's decision. It merely means, for whatever reason, that the Court does not choose to hear the issue at that time.

The state court systems operate much like the federal system. The lower courts hear the evidence and make decisions of fact and law, and then the appeals courts review the record and determine whether there have been any mistakes that must be corrected. Each state has different names for its various courts, but all have at least three levels, with a supreme-type court having the final word if the court chooses to hear the case. The highest court in each state is the ultimate decider of issues involving state laws and state constitutions. Even the United States Supreme Court cannot overturn a state court in these matters, unless there is also an issue involving the United States Constitution. Often, however, as is the case in the area of sexual harassment, state courts will look to the federal court's decisions in a parallel federal law area for assistance in deciding cases under their own state laws. Title VII decisions are often used by state courts in interpreting their own states' civil rights acts.

The Types of Laws

Both federal and state courts are involved in deciding cases in the three categories of law found in every state but Louisiana: constitutional, statutory, and common law. Constitutional cases involve interpretation and application of either the state or the federal Constitution, depending on the court system. Statutory law involves the interpretation and application of laws, often termed *acts,* passed by the legislative bodies: Congress in the federal system and the state legislatures in the state system. There are both federal and state statutes dealing with employment discrimination. At the national level, the law is contained in Title VII, a section of the Civil Rights Act of 1964.

Common law is more complex than statutory law and requires more explanation. Common law is, in effect, judge-made law. Throughout the history of the English and United States courts, various disputes that were not covered by any statutory or constitutional dictates have arisen between parties. The judges in these cases have been called upon to settle the disputes and, in doing so, make decisions about various issues in each case. For example, these issues include the duties owed by members of society to others in the community, the extent of liability of a person committing a "wrongful act," the damages that must be paid, the point at which a contract is formed, and the effect of various events on liability. As these cases were decided, a series of precedents were set, which other courts could or must (if set by a higher court) follow when deciding cases involving the same issues. As new cases presented new situations and additional issues, the law developed into a complex system called the *common law.* Thus common law is involved in almost every legal dispute that does not involve either a statute or a constitution. Although there is some federal common law in areas in which the federal courts have jurisdiction, common-law cases are normally heard in state courts.

> *An example of a common-law claim is the one that Fred heard about in the case study—the employee is claiming that the supervisor intentionally inflicted emotional distress on her and caused her damage. This is a type of* tort *lawsuit—a lawsuit brought by a private party for damages sustained because of the actions of another private party.*

As will be seen later with regard to the law of sexual harassment, even though a statute may allow a person to bring a statutory lawsuit against someone, there still may be common-law claims that can be brought along with that claim. Statutory and common-law claims may be brought together if the facts support both.

The Hierarchy of Laws

Just as there is a hierarchy in the court system, there is also a hierarchy in the types of laws. Common law is the lowest-level law, and any common-law decision that is in conflict with a statutory or constitutional rule is no longer good law. Thus, as often occurs, if a legislative body does not like a common-law precedent, it can pass a statute that will overturn the common law. No statute can overturn a constitutional mandate, however, because the constitution is the highest law, superseding all others. Whereas the state constitution is normally the ultimate law in each state, the United States Constitution supersedes all laws, including each state's constitution.

The Interplay of State and Federal Laws

In addition to concerns about the hierarchy of the types of law, there are also issues regarding the hierarchy between state and federal laws. When conflict appears between the state and federal laws, a decision must be made as to which law preempts or supersedes the other.

before buy

> *An example of this problem can be seen in the case study, where a state has attempted to change the federal law of sexual harassment by specifically protecting the use of girlie calendars and magazines in the workplace. In that situation, a court would have to determine whether the federal law or the state law should be enforced.*

Although preemption cases can be very complex and sometimes must be decided by the United States Supreme Court, it is possible to state a few general rules about when federal law will preempt a conflicting state law. First, the laws that are in conflict must involve an area in which the United States Constitution grants power to the federal government. Second, in order for preemption to exist, either (1) the federal government must have shown an intent to "occupy the field," in other words, not to allow states to regulate in this area, or (2) the state law must be in conflict with the federal law.

Federal antidiscrimination laws are passed by Congress, largely under the power granted to it by Article 8 of the United States Constitution (often called the Commerce Clause) to regulate interstate commerce. Through a series of Supreme Court cases involving the extent of this power, Congress has been interpreted to have authority to regulate activity that has a substantial effect, directly or indirectly and individually or collectively, on interstate commerce. Although there have been challenges to laws such as the Civil Rights Act of 1964, the Supreme Court has refused to overturn Congress's finding that discrimination with regard to employment and accommodations would have a substantial effect on interstate commerce. Thus it has been decided that the federal government has the power to regulate various types of discrimination.

Does federal law then automatically preempt state laws dealing with discrimination? Recall that the issue requires one further analysis step. Title VII specifically states that Congress did not intend to occupy the field of employment-discrimination law, and thus states may pass laws of their own, which may in fact be even stricter than the federal law. Several states, for example, have laws that allow greater damages than does Title VII, and those laws are not preempted, a reason why many employees who have been sexually harassed choose to pursue both a federal and a state law claim when possible.

With regard to the possibility of preemption, however, a state may not enforce a law that conflicts with the federal law, and any law that legalizes behavior that the federal law prohibits would do just that. Thus the pornographic pictures in the case study would have to go.

Another aspect of the U.S. legal system that is important in a complete understanding of the law of sexual harassment involves the "reach" of statutory laws or, in other words, who must obey them. Most federal and state laws will specify the individuals covered by the statute. For example, Title VII covers employers, labor organizations, and employment agencies, as well as their agents, and specifically defines those terms for purposes of the act. State laws may regulate only individuals or companies over which the state has jurisdiction. This usually means those who live or do business in the state. Federal laws may regulate not only any individual in the United States but also, in some situations, individuals who are in foreign countries. Title VII presents an interesting example of this extraterritorial jurisdiction, and the history of the application of the law presents a classic example of how legislatures can change some court decisions.

In early 1991, the United States Supreme Court decided the case of *EEOC v. Arabian American Oil Co.,*[1] in which an American citizen claimed that he was discriminated against by his employer, a United States company, while he was working for the company in a foreign country. Although the Supreme Court decided that it was within the power of Congress to regulate this activity as long as it involved a U.S. company, the Court nonetheless decided that Congress did not intend such an application. In October 1991, Congress amended Title VII to make it clear that it did intend that U.S. nationals working in foreign offices of U.S. companies be protected from discrimination. Thus, Title VII now regulates activity both inside and outside the United States when the employer is a U.S. company and the employee is a U.S. national.

The Role of Precedent

Precedent is important in the American legal system, both in the common law and in statutory or constitutional interpretation. When a court is presented with an issue to decide, there are probably several previously decided cases that involved issues much like those in the current case. Using a legal doctrine called *stare decisis,* a court will usually follow the previous decisions, unless there is some strong reason to change the course of the law. A court must follow any applicable precedents that were set by courts classified as higher courts.

Federal district courts in each region must adhere to the precedents set in their own circuit court of appeals but are not required to follow rules set in other circuits. In addition, no circuit court of appeals is bound by the decisions of another circuit court. Many of the sexual harassment cases that will be discussed in the following chapters are decisions of the various circuit courts of appeals.

Even though a circuit court opinion does not establish precedent for another circuit's court, all courts in the federal system are required to follow the decisions of the United States Supreme Court, the highest court in the federal system. The Supreme Court has the final say in all matters involving interpretation of federal laws and the federal Constitution.

In response to Fred's question in the case study, the courts where his case will be heard will have already decided several cases with regard to how egregious behavior must be in order to fit under the "intentional infliction of emotional distress" claim. His attorney will be looking into those cases to see what the rules and facts in the previous decisions can tell Fred about the possible outcome in his case. This could help him in deciding whether to settle the case or go to court.

The Role of Government Agencies

The role of government agencies in the United States legal system must also be reviewed for a complete understanding of the law of sexual harassment. The laws that govern how agencies operate and the regulations that such agencies create are usually referred to as *administrative law.*

Although many volumes have been and can be written about administrative law, some general principles are adequate to understand the role of the agencies involved in the discrimination arena. First, agencies are given power only when it is delegated by another branch of government. This usually means that Congress or a state legislative body delegates some of its power, in what is called an *enabling act,* to an agency that is then enabled to carry out certain specified functions. Although this power is legislative, agencies may also have some executive and judicial power. Depending on the specific provisions of its enabling act, an agency may perform a variety of functions. It may promulgate regulations that create new rights and responsibilities in its particular area of expertise. An agency may issue interpretations of specific provisions of the laws over which it has been delegated authority. These interpretations are usually termed *guidelines.* An agency may hold hearings on issues of importance, make recommendations to Congress or the state legislatures, investigate possible violations of the laws, issue violation notices, hold hearings to determine liability, and assess damages.

As is obvious, agencies have a great deal of influence in the development of law in the United States, but like all government entities, they are subject to limitations. Agencies may not go beyond the powers granted to them in their enabling act, and any action taken by them, including interpreting laws and promulgating regulations, is subject to challenge in the courts. If the courts feel, for example, that an agency has misinterpreted the law in a guideline, they may overturn the interpretation. Usually, however, the courts give a great deal of deference to an agency determination because the agency has special expertise in the area under consideration. In addition, agency processes are controlled by the dictates of the Administrative Procedures Act, which sets out requirements for many agency actions.

The agency involved in Title VII cases is the Equal Employment Opportunity Commission, and most states that have civil rights laws have their own antidiscrimination agencies. The EEOC has specific powers granted to it by Congress in a variety of laws, including the Civil Rights Act of 1964, the Americans with Disabilities Act, and the Equal Pay Act. These powers include the ability to issue guidelines, investigate complaints, mediate disputes, and bring lawsuits to court. The EEOC has been involved in many cases in the area of sexual harassment and has had a strong influence on the development of law in this area. A more detailed description of the EEOC and its investigative process is included in chapter 6.

Alternate Dispute Resolution

Many employers are attempting to stop complaints of discrimination from coming to court by asking employees to enter into arbitration agreements. These agreements require that any claim, including those involving sexual harassment, be submitted to an arbitrator or arbitration panel before a court becomes involved. There is some recent evidence that the EEOC will challenge arbitration agreements if they are a precondition to getting or keeping a job. Whereas the validity of arbitration agreements in this area is not absolutely clear, it does appear that at least voluntary agreements may be enforceable if adequate measures are included to protect the rights of the complainants. This would include making sure that the employee knows exactly what she or he is signing.

Such agreements cannot circumvent the law, however, and will probably not stop lawsuits, even if arbitration is pursued first. They can be useful, though, especially with regard to the cost savings and the relative speed of the decision making, and will probably be used more frequently in the future. Anyone considering such an agreement should involve an experienced attorney in the process. Doing so will ensure that any recent court decisions have been followed and that adequate provisions are provided to uphold the agreement's validity.

Summary

The United States system of jurisprudence involves a variety of different types of laws and two parallel court systems, each with its own jurisdiction and precedents. All of these types of laws and both the federal and state courts may be involved in a sexual harassment case, and understanding how the laws and courts operate can be helpful in understanding what to expect in such a situation.

For Reflection

1. Discuss the three types of law found in all states except Louisiana and how each type of law originates.
2. Explain the concept of preemption. Why is it so important in sexual harassment cases?
3. Discuss the problems that may be encountered in adding an arbitration clause to an employment contract.
4. What is the EEOC? Where does it fit in the legal system? Where does it get its power? If Congress does not like a regulation that the EEOC promulgates, can Congress overturn it? If so, how?

Notes

1. EEOC v. Arabian American Oil Co., 499 U.S. 244 (1991).

CHAPTER **2**

Sexual Harassment from the Legal Perspective

In trying to review what we have had before us, it strikes me that we have taken on a question that, by any measure, is very difficult. It is not just that we have had two very persuasive people before us, but I have tried to make some notes as to what it is we are looking at. We are looking at a very serious charge. We are looking at a charge about activities, about very repugnant statements of an extreme nature, and the case is one where there are no witnesses.

—Senator Brown,
Senate Judiciary Confirmation Hearings
of Clarence Thomas, 1991

CASE STUDY

Victoria Janus and Marjorie Mattis are the only women who work in the maintenance department at Consolidated Dermatics. One morning, they arrive at work to find that a pinup picture of Marjorie, which she posed for many years earlier, has been placed over the workbench of Fred Fandes, one of the other workers. Marjorie asks him to remove it, but he refuses.

Victoria wants to complain to the boss, but Marjorie urges her to forget it because "it will only make things worse." Victoria decides to approach her boss, Mark Steel, anyway, but he tells her, "One little picture won't hurt you, and if Marjorie would stop wearing such short skirts, this would never have happened." When Victoria tells Marjorie about the response, Marjorie is not surprised. "Don't forget," Marjorie reminds her, "Fred is Henrietta Fandes's brother, and she's the VP of this division." "That's right," responds Victoria, "and Mark would never upset Henrietta because he got his job only because he's sleeping with her."

Would Victoria and Marjorie have a legal case against Consolidated Dermatics for sexual harassment? Would the facts that Marjorie posed for the picture and that Marjorie dresses in a "sexy" manner have an effect on a potential case? Has Mark been sexually harassed?

Introduction

Federal and state statutes passed by Congress or state legislatures form the foundation for the laws against sexual harassment in the workplace in the United States. As noted in chapter 1, the applicable federal statute is Title VII, part of the Civil Rights Act of 1964. Most states also have civil rights laws that deal with sexual harassment and that apply to businesses in those states. In addition, in many sexual harassment cases, the plaintiffs also file traditional common-law claims against an employer or a harasser. These claims may include allegations such as intentional or negligent infliction of emotional distress, assault, battery, or negligent hiring or retention. These claims are often allowed to be filed along with a claim under the state and federal laws and, at times, can result in damage awards even higher than those allowed in the statutes. The outcome of such common-law claims usually depends on a finding of liability for sexual harassment under the statutory law. For that reason, and because such claims are covered by traditional common-law tort standards, common-law claims will not be extensively covered in this book. A basic text on business law can help in providing further understanding.

The Statutory Framework

Generally, the federal law covers only people working for a business with fifteen or more employees, but many state laws cover smaller businesses.[1] In Michigan, for example, any employer with one or more employees must follow the requirements of that state's civil rights statute. Thus most businesses in today's environment are covered by one or more of these laws. Although state laws differ in some aspects from the federal law, state courts often use federal cases as precedent for interpretations of their own state statutes. This practice means that Title VII often sets the standards in the area of sexual harassment law.

The wording of Title VII is quite simple. It states that it is illegal to "fail or refuse to hire or to discharge any individual" or to discriminate in the "compensation, terms, conditions or privileges of employment" on the basis of an employee's or prospective employee's race, color, religion, sex, or national origin. It is the courts' ever-expanding interpretation of the term *discrimination* that has made the area of discrimination more complex.

In the U.S. legal system, it is the role of the courts to interpret legislative actions or statutes and to decide when and how laws should apply in individual cases. Sexual harassment lawsuits continue to present courts with a variety of opportunities to make such determinations.

Defining Sexual Harassment

It is not easy to state an exact, understandable, and workable definition of sexual harassment. The Equal Employment Opportunity Commission (EEOC), the federal agency designated by Title VII to interpret the law and handle employment discrimination complaints, has attempted to define sexual harassment using the following language:

> Unwelcome sexual advances, requests for sexual favors, and other verbal or physical conduct of a sexual nature constitute sexual harassment when (1) submission to such conduct is made either explicitly or implicitly a term or condition of an individual's employment, (2) submission to or rejection of such conduct by an individual is used as the basis for employment decisions affecting such individual, or (3) such conduct has the purpose or effect of unreasonably interfering with an individual's work performance or creating an intimidating, hostile, or offensive working environment.

The EEOC issued this definition on the basis of the commission's authority under Title VII to interpret the parameters of discrimination on the basis of sex. The EEOC has realized, however, that this original definition is incomplete. Recently, it proposed a modification that would make the definition more consistent with the results in recent cases.

In its proposed new guidelines, the EEOC first wanted to make it clear that conduct does not necessarily have to interfere with an individual's work performance in order for it to violate Title VII. This would have been accomplished by adding the words "or otherwise adversely affects an individual's employment opportunities" to part 3 of the current definition. Second, the agency wanted to make it clear that it interpreted Title VII to prohibit any gender-based harassment, even though it may not be sexual in nature. Thus behavior that has no overt sexual overtones but that "denigrates or shows hostility or aversion toward a person because of their gender" would be illegal. Unfortunately, because of a controversy that erupted about the part of the guidelines that interpreted religious harassment, the agency withdrew the guidelines, intending to reissue them at a later date. Although the new guidelines were withdrawn, current EEOC practices and court decisions make it clear that the proposed sexual harassment wording reflected current interpretations and will continue to be part of the law.

The EEOC definition, although often quoted, is not of great help in understanding exactly what behavior is covered or how a responsible employer should deal with potential problems. Nonetheless, many businesses feel that merely quoting the EEOC definition in a policy is adequate to avoid liability, even though most employees and even managers don't have a clue as to what the definition means. Unfortunately, understanding is the key to dealing with sexual harassment in the workplace, and this why it is important to go beyond the EEOC definition and look more closely at the entire issue of sexual harassment.

The Two Types of Sexual Harassment

There are two types of sexual harassment situations described by the EEOC definition: *quid pro quo* and hostile or discriminatory work environment. The United States Supreme Court has agreed with the agency that both of these are violations of the federal law. Because the two types involve different conduct and have their own legal parameters, each must be looked at separately.

QUID PRO QUO HARASSMENT

The first sexual harassment cases involved what has been termed a *quid pro quo* situation. *Quid pro quo* is a legal term, most often used in contract cases, that roughly translates to "something for something." In a contract case this means that each party must receive some benefit in order for there to be a binding agreement. Under the EEOC definition, *quid pro quo* cases involve behavior in which "submission to such conduct is made either explicitly or implicitly a term or condition of an individual's employment [or] submission to or rejection of such conduct by an individual is used as the basis for employment decisions affecting such individual."

The Elements of a *Quid Pro Quo* Claim Basically, in a *quid pro quo* case the employee is claiming that a supervisor or someone with authority to confer workplace benefits is offering those benefits in exchange for sexual favors or is threatening to take away economic benefits if the employee does not accept the "offer." As the law is defined, this places a discriminatory condition on the employee; terms of employment are being changed because of her or his gender. In short, in *quid pro quo* situations, because of their sex, employees are being forced to comply with conditions that other workers do not face.

In order to be illegal, the "offer" in a *quid pro quo* case must be "unwelcomed" by the employee. This requirement basically means that the employee did not want to be subjected to this "choice." Whereas this is rarely an issue in *quid pro quo* cases, it does become more relevant in hostile-environment situations and will be discussed later in this chapter in that context.

Quid pro quo cases were being filed as early as the 1970s. One of the most influential was *Barnes v. Costle,*[2] a lawsuit that alleged that a supervisor was instrumental in abolishing an employee's position because she spurned his sexual advances. The court found that the employee was presented with an offer—continued employment for sexual favors—and suffered a loss of her job because she did not accept. In *Barnes,* the court agreed with the EEOC's interpretation that this behavior violated Title VII and set down guidelines for deciding such cases. Whereas most harassment cases are brought by women, when men do claim sexual harassment, it usually involves *quid pro quo* harassment rather than a hostile-environment claim.

Since *Barnes,* the courts have been unanimous in allowing these types of lawsuits. Because they involve blatantly illegal behavior, *quid pro quo* cases have proven relatively simple for the courts to decide. The biggest issue becomes a determination of fact, that is, whether this illegal bargain was in fact proposed and, usually, whether it was the basis of the detriment suffered by the plaintiff.

While most *quid pro quo* cases have involved an employee who suffered a workplace detriment because she or he did not go along with the illegal behavior, an interesting new situation is beginning to appear in court cases. This involves instances where an "offer" is made, yet the subordinate employee did not suffer adverse circumstances. This could be because (1) the plaintiff gave in to the advances, (2) the person with the power advantage was still "negotiating," or (3) the perpetrator did not carry through with the expected response.

At least one court has stated that these "offer with no detrimental consequences" situations can still be tried as *quid pro quo* cases. In 1994, in *Karibian v. Columbia University,*[3] the United States Court of Appeals for the Second Circuit decided that requiring an "actual economic loss" in these cases would place "undue emphasis on the victim's response to the sexual harassment. It believed that the focus should be on the prohibited conduct, not the victim's reaction."[4] Consequently, the court was looking at the illegal proposal rather than the denial of some benefit as the discriminatory treatment and decided that the law was broken by the "unwelcomed" offer itself.

It must be noted that the EEOC has not specifically commented on the use of a *quid pro quo* claim in *Karibian*-type situations. In the law, however, such cases sometimes signal a new trend, which the agency and other courts may choose to adopt. Currently, though, the EEOC and most courts would treat such situations as hostile or work environment cases, the second type of sexual harassment discussed in this chapter.

> *In the case study, it is alleged that Mark Steel received his job as the benefit in a* quid pro quo *offer. This presents a situation much like that in* Karibian. *Mark does not appear to have suffered any detriment here. If the offer was "unwelcomed" by him, however, and the court in which his case is tried accepts the view that the offer itself is a violation of Title VII, Mark could still have a* quid pro quo *harassment lawsuit against the company.*

Employer Liability for *Quid Pro Quo* Harassment   There is at least one reason why an employer would not want a lawsuit tried as a *quid pro quo* case, rather than one alleging another type of harassment. When a claim of *quid pro quo* harassment is proven, the employer will be subject to a harsher standard with regard to the employer's liability for the actions of its employees. Basically this means that there is no defense, even if the employer has taken all possible steps to stop this from happening. The law calls this *strict liability,* the application of which is not based on fault or intentional or negligent behavior but because someone has to pay for the damages, and it should be those who hired and retained this person.

Obviously, *quid pro quo* cases do present a significant problem for an employer and romantic advances and dating by supervisors or those in authority have the potential to cause great difficulty. Are work benefits or threats of detrimental consequences part of these relationships? It is the employer's responsibility to know and to deal with such situations.

Additionally, with regard to a supervisor and subordinate's dating, it is possible that a relationship that a supervisor views as consensual may actually be based on the power differential. Does the employee feel that workplace decisions about her or his compensation, conditions, terms, or privileges of employment may be affected because of her or his response to a request for dates, lunches, or more, even if this is not the case? Despite the fact that there may be no direct promise or threat, the situation may cause an employee to feel that she or he has no choice but to enter into an unwanted relationship with a person who has authority over her or him. Also, a relationship between people of differing power positions in the company is fraught with the potential of future problems when decisions must be made about promotions, raises, days off, and every conceivable workplace matter.

Managers should be strongly advised against becoming involved with anyone with less power or authority in the workplace, as this situation has the potential to cause extensive problems for them, the employees, and the employer. In addition, as is the case now in many workplaces, behavior such as relationships with or dating of subordinates is becoming part of the evaluation of a manager's performance. Such conduct by managers, when they are educated on the problem, displays poor managerial judgment and unsatisfactory management skills.

HOSTILE OR WORK ENVIRONMENT HARASSMENT

Quid pro quo sexual harassment is present only when there is an illegal and unwelcome negotiation going on between people of unequal authority in the workplace. Harassment can occur even when this is not the case. Behavior or conduct by an employee's peers, as well as by superiors when *quid pro quo* is not proven, could be the basis of an even more complex sexual harassment lawsuit: one alleging that the employer maintains a work environment that denies equal employment opportunity.

Discriminatory work environment cases fit under the last part of the EEOC definition of sexual harassment: unwelcome conduct that "has the purpose or effect of unreasonably interfering with an individual's work performance or creating an intimidating, hostile, or offensive working environment." Current practice and court decisions, as well as the new guidelines if they are reissued and adopted, also include a situation where the behavior "otherwise adversely affects an individual's employment opportunities." It is this type of case that is most often involved when the term *sexual harassment* is used now and that is the basis of most of the confusion with regard to what is appropriate and legal in workplaces today.

Work environment sexual harassment cases are far more complex than *quid pro quo* lawsuits and cause a variety of problems for courts and government agencies, as well as for employers. Because it is a fairly new area of the law, its exact parameters continue to evolve and the definition appears to change daily. Most of these cases are brought by women, and after further reading in this chapter and the next, it will become clear why.

Trade journals and business publications are often reporting on new cases that stretch what was once thought to be the limits of liability in this area. Daily, courts are being faced with cases involving behavior that some had once viewed as appropriate and assigning liability that had not been expected. After the hearings on allegations of sexual harassment against then-Justice-elect Clarence Thomas, *Business Week* noted that the rules were changing faster than most people could comprehend:

> A revolution in the law on sexual harassment underlies all the hubbub over Thomas and Hill. It was as recently as 1980 that the Equal Employment Opportunity Commission first identified two types of sexual harassment. Companies easily understand the obvious kind: Sleep with me, honey, or you're fired. But they often don't quite get the murkier, second form: hostile environment harassment. Here, as in the Thomas affair, questionable behavior may be subtle

and cumulative, ranging from lewd jokes to nude calendars or even obsessive staring. Now, courts are ruling that the conduct has to be judged, not by the old "reasonable man" rule, but from the eyes of a "reasonable woman." And they're stretching the definition so fast that many employers can't keep up.[5]

Business Week is describing is what is termed in the legal world as "hostile or intimidating work environment" harassment. Unfortunately, this legal term is neither particularly useful nor clear. It appears to be describing a workplace where vigilantes are roaming about with guns looking for workers to harass, yet much more subtle behavior, which many might not regard as hostile or intimidating, can also be the basis of a work environment sexual harassment claim. A clearer and more descriptive term is *discriminatory work environment* because the basis of these claims is that some behavior, conduct, work rule, or a combination of these has created an environment that makes it more difficult for workers of one gender to be successful. Because many workplaces have been traditionally male dominated, at least at the power or decision-making levels, it is argued that they are often structured in a way that makes it conducive to male success. This means that most of these types of cases will involve, and in fact do involve, a claim that the environment inhibits women from equal opportunity.

Pivotal Hostile Environment Cases   At first, because of the complex psychological issues involved in determining what creates an environment that is less conducive to the success of one gender than the other, courts were reticent to become involved in work-environment sexual harassment cases.

Although many lower federal courts had agreed with the EEOC definition and the use of Title VII for such cases before 1986, it was not until that year that the United States Supreme Court agreed that a sexually discriminatory work environment, in fact, fit within Title VII's prohibition of discrimination on the basis of sex. In the famous case of *Meritor Savings Bank v. Vinson,*[6] the Supreme Court decided that the EEOC was correct in its interpretation that Title VII was intended to cover discriminatory work-environment situations. *Vinson* involved outrageous behavior by a Sidney Taylor, a bank supervisor, who forced intercourse on the plaintiff, as well as exposing himself to her and other employees. Taylor had not explicitly or implicitly made an offer of workplace benefits, however. The lower court had decided that this conduct still violated Title VII because it created a hostile work environment for women.

The Supreme Court stated in *Vinson* that it agreed that certain conduct, directed toward women, whether or not it is directly linked to the grant or denial of an economic benefit, could constitute a violation of Title VII if the conduct "has the purpose or effect of unreasonably interfering with an individual's work performance or creating an intimidating, hostile, or offensive working environment."[7]

Since the *Vinson* case, courts have grappled with the problem of when workplace behavior crosses over the boundaries of Title VII. Although *Vinson* may have sent shock waves through the business community, it merely signaled the beginning of a complex and continuing determination as to the line between appropriate and hostile or intimidating behavior. In the years since *Vinson,* that line has been continually changing to recognize that what was once normal workplace behavior is, in reality, illegal sexual harassment.

In the early cases, it appeared that only overtly abusive behavior would result in a finding that there was a discriminatory or hostile work environment. For example, the Supreme Court noted in a later decision that the *Vinson* case involved "appalling conduct" and some "especially egregious examples of harassment."[8] Mechelle Vinson was subjected to intense abuse by her supervisor, and it was clear under any standard that the environment in which Ms. Vinson worked was abusive and hostile.

Courts began to find, however, that conduct that was not so overtly abusive could also create a problem environment. In 1991 the ninth circuit court of appeals found discrimination in a situation that presented what could be viewed as a much less abusive environment. The case, *Ellison v. Brady,*[9] involved a co-worker's continuing "romantic" overtures to Kerry Ellison, an employee of the Internal Revenue Service. There were no threats or physical contact between the two workers. The man involved expressed his interest in a relationship in writing on two or three occasions, and in conversations he "pester[ed] her with unnecessary questions."[10]

Even though the behavior of the co-worker in *Ellison* may have seemed to the managers in charge to be merely annoying and not of the type that would cause legal liability, they found that they were wrong. Although the district court deemed the behavior "trivial and isolated" and, in essence, determined that such behavior was part of the dating ritual, the appeals court specifically decided, when it viewed the situation from the perspective of women in the society, that a hostile environment had been created for Ms. Ellison. This *reasonable woman* perspective will be discussed later in this chapter.

In this case, the employer's negligent handling of the situation, perhaps because it was relying on the fact that previous cases had required a more intense level of harassment for liability, resulted in extensive liability. Ms. Ellison's employer should not have been surprised. What is clear is that any list of conduct that could lead to problems is not exhaustive. As the *Ellison* court specifically stated when discussing the type of behavior that creates a discriminatory work environment, "Our examples are illustrative and not exclusive because we realize that sexual harassment is a rapidly expanding area of the law."[11]

In 1991, the United States Supreme Court reviewed hostile environment cases and agreed that behavior that was not nearly as abusive as that of the supervisor in *Vinson* could still violate Title VII. In *Harris v. Forklift Systems,*[12] the court had to decide how serious behavior must be in order to violate Title

VII. Some lower courts had been applying a standard that appeared to require that conduct be intense enough to "seriously affect the psychological well-being" of the plaintiff.[13] This amounted, in some cases, to a requirement that the employee have suffered a serious psychological injury.

The Supreme Court in *Harris* rejected such a requirement and made it clear that there cannot be a "mathematically precise test" for determining how intense harassment had to be to create a hostile environment. Because of the wide range of potential behaviors and the infinite variations of harassment, the Court stated that it could not formulate an exact statement as to what conduct does or does not result in illegal sexual harassment. The Court did note, however, that "Title VII comes into play before the harassment leads to a nervous breakdown."[14]

Although the Supreme Court was not especially clear about the exact *types* or *amount* of behavior that would create a hostile environment, the Court did state that certain *effects* might be expected when behavior had crossed the line:

> A discriminatorily abusive work environment, even one that does not seriously affect employees' psychological well-being, can and often will detract from employees' job performance, discourage employees from remaining on the job, or keep them from advancing in their careers.[15]

As is the case with all lists in this area of the law, however, this list of effects is not exhaustive. As the Supreme Court itself knew, it would be foolish to think that these are the only effects that might be expected. Looking at any one benchmark, such as whether there is a measurable decrease in an employee's job performance, may not be helpful. As Justice Ginsberg noted in her concurrence in *Harris,* a decrease in tangible work productivity is not necessary for the environment to be discriminatory. The best course is to look at, as the Supreme Court directed, the totality of the circumstances with regard to each case.

The Elements of a Hostile Environment Claim   It is clear that there are no easy answers in this area of the law. Even the Supreme Court appears to know more about what *effect* illegal behavior will have than about the type or severity of behavior needed to create a discriminatory work environment. In the end, a court or jury will have to decide, based on the unique circumstances in each case, whether Title VII has been violated in any particular situation.

There are some guidelines, however, that are helpful in making a determination as to whether there is, legally speaking, a hostile environment in a workplace. These guidelines have been developed through precedents in a variety of cases, and a set of standards has begun to emerge. In general, these require that the harassing behavior or conduct be proven (1) to be gender based, (2) to affect a term or condition of employment, and (3) to be "unwelcomed."

Is the Harassing Conduct Based on Gender?   As has been stated, sexual harassment, in its legal use, means conduct that *discriminates* in some way against a worker on the basis of her or his gender. Because the harassment must be *discriminatory* in order to violate Title VII or any state law that designates gender as a protected category, the behavior or the environment created by the behavior must have the purpose or effect of making success on the job more difficult for *one* gender than the other.

The conduct that creates an unequal opportunity for success does not need to be sexual in nature, although often it is. Physical or verbal conduct that is gender based and that belittles or demeans an employee is sexual harassment, whether or not it has a sexual connotation. Calling someone a "dumb-assed woman," as the supervisor did in *Harris,* could be argued to have no sexual connotation. In a legal sense, however, it is sexually or gender based and would be viewed as sexual harassment.

It is perhaps not too difficult to see that overtly belittling behavior or demeaning comments directed at those of one gender, rather than the other, would viewed as gender based. The statements are made because of the person's gender. Thus, when someone of one gender is adversely treated or is subject to epithets or comments that are not directed at workers of the other gender, this criterion is satisfied.

What is more difficult to understand, however, is the situation where all workers are subjected to the same behavior, but the effect is different because of a person's gender. Although it could be stated, on one hand, that these sorts of behavior and displays are not discriminatory because both men and women must see and hear them, many courts have determined that the effect is quite different for men and women. We will discuss this issue later in this chapter and more fully in the next chapter, because it involves the complex interplay of psychology and socialization. Legally speaking, however, it will suffice to say that this element is also satisfied when the court or jury finds that the environment, because of differences in male and female perceptions, is "uniquely hostile to one gender" or interferes with the terms or conditions of employment of one gender.

Are Conditions of Employment Affected?   In order to violate Title VII, the harassment must be more than "trivial." It must be severe enough to alter the conditions of employment. It is in this area that the real difference is found between conduct that is legally harassment and conduct that is just realistically harassment. Thus an isolated incident of harassment, while obviously behavior that harasses, may not be considered severe enough to reach the level of creating a hostile or discriminatory work environment.

As the Supreme Court noted in *Vinson,* "not all workplace conduct that may be described as 'harassment' affects 'a term, condition, or privilege' of employment within the meaning of Title VII."[16] Thus, in order to meet the legal standard, the harassment must be seen as "sufficiently severe or pervasive to alter the conditions of the [the victim's] employment and create an abusive working environment." In *Harris,* the Supreme Court discussed this requirement, stating that certain evidence should be examined, even though it made clear that no one individual circumstance was key:

> [W]e can say that whether an environment is "hostile" or "abusive" can be determined only by looking at all the circumstances. These may include the frequency of the discriminatory conduct; its severity; whether it is physically threatening or humiliating, or a mere offensive utterance; and whether it unreasonably interferes with an employee's work performance.[17]

What is clear is that individual behavior that might be deemed not to meet this criterion, if combined with other conduct or the wrong response by the company, can be elevated into a situation where employment conditions are altered. As one court noted:

> [A] holistic perspective is necessary, keeping in mind that each successive episode has its predecessors, that the impact of the separate incidents may accumulate, and that the work environment created thereby may exceed the sum of the individual episodes.[18]

> *The case study presents an interesting situation with regard to this element of a hostile-environment case. Is the one instance of harassing behavior, the picture of Marjorie, severe enough to be said to alter the conditions of employment? Would the company's lack of adequate response and the supervisor's comments raise it to the level of a hostile or discriminatory work environment? It is possible that this might be the case.*

The determination of when behavior reaches a level of severity or seriousness as to alter the conditions of employment is often complex and involves many of the same explorations used in deciding whether an environment is gender based. Because of uniqueness between the sexes, some workplace conduct may not have the same effect on men and women. An understanding of complex psychological issues is often needed in order to make a correct determination as to whether the abusiveness of an environment has reached the level of being called legally discriminatory.

It is interesting to note that courts often rely heavily on sociological and psychological testimony about the effects of certain behavior to help them in making a decision as to whether the conditions of employment have been affected. Studies done by psychologists and sociologists and their testimony as expert witnesses have been instrumental in moving the courts to recognize that when the effect of behavior is understood, conduct that might appear at first glance to be trivial may in fact reach the level of creating a discriminatory work environment. This is why what was in the past deemed workplace fun may today be illegal harassment.

Effect vs. Intent   The EEOC has always interpreted the law to require that the effect and not the intent of harassing behavior be the important consideration in determining whether a term or condition of employment is affected. Lower courts and the Supreme Court in the *Harris* case agreed with this interpretation. A discriminatory environment is created not by what is in the mind of the person carrying out the behavior but rather by what effect it has on the person viewing the behavior.

This effect versus intent focus is difficult for many people in the workplace to understand and accept. Whereas some workers who harass may be well aware that they are using certain behavior in order to cause problems or to victimize those with whom they are not comfortable in the workplace, others may actually be acting on subconscious feelings of anxiety or anger. Workers, for example, may display sexual posters for a variety of reasons and will resist any suggestion that they are harassing others, even if their underlying motive is, in fact, to make another feel uncomfortable and out of place. Still others may not believe that certain behavior is a problem because it is how the workplace has always been structured. Not understanding differing perspectives, they may be totally unaware of the effect that their behavior has on others.

It is vital that everyone in the workplace be made to recognize that it is not the intent of the behavior that is important nor the fact that some may not view the environment as hostile, abusive, or offensive. What is important is the effect of the conduct on other workers.

In order to determine whether a term or condition of employment has been affected, the courts will not be concerned with whether anyone had a discriminatory motive. They will be looking to see whether this behavior would have a detrimental effect on a reasonable person *and* whether it had an effect on this plaintiff. These are called the *objective* and *subjective* tests.

The Objective Test   A determination of when an environment reaches the discriminatory level requires that the courts use an objective test with regard to the effect of conduct or behavior. Although some people may find even the most "trivial" behavior offensive, it is clear that the decision as to whether terms or conditions of employment have been changed must be made using an objective perspective: that of an average or reasonable, and not a hypersensitive, individual. Would a reasonable person be affected? As courts are finding out, this decision is often dependent on whose perspective is used: a reasonable woman or a reasonable man.

Often, a court will find that the first decision it must make in a sexual harassment case is what perspective must be used in order to determine whether behavior has had the effect of affecting a term or condition of employment. Because psychologists report that men and women experience, view, react to, and deal with behaviors differently, the same conduct, if viewed from the perspective of a reasonable woman, may have quite a different effect than if judged from the perspective of the reasonable man. There are a variety of reasons put forward for this differing perspective, many involving differing socialization, some of which will be dealt with more extensively in chapter 3.

A determination as to whether a situation is viewed through the eyes of a man or a woman will make a great deal of difference to the outcome of a case. The next chapter will explain this phenomenon in more psychological terms, terms that are being heard more and more in court proceedings and that are having a great influence on the shape of the law of sexual harassment.

Although the Supreme Court has stated that it is important that an objective view of the environment be used to judge whether it is discriminatory, the Court has not made clear whether this objective view is male or female oriented or some combination of the two. Thus, lower courts are free to make this determination on their own.

As we previously discussed, the *Ellison* court specifically stated that it was viewing the conduct directed at Ms. Ellison through the eyes of a reasonable woman and determined that this resulted in a verdict for the plaintiff. It further stated that this was the only correct way to decide these cases and directed the courts in the ninth circuit to use the "reasonable woman" standard in sexual harassment lawsuits involving a female plaintiff and a claim of "hostile environment." Many other courts have also taken this step, including the courts in *Lipsett v. University of Puerto Rico,*[19] *Andrews v. City of Philadelphia,*[20] and *Burns v. McGregor Electronic Industries.*[21]

Although the term *reasonable person* may seem gender neutral, claims have been made that the traditional reasonable person is in fact male oriented. Some, including the courts that have adopted the differing perspective standard, claim that any other approach would disregard the law's intent. One judge noted that not viewing the behavior from the perspective of the gender being subjected to the harassment would permit employers to "sustain ingrained notions of reasonable behavior fashioned by the offenders."[22]

Because the trend is definitely toward a gender-specific standard and because the key to a finding of liability in these cases is proof that the workplace creates an environment that disadvantages one gender over the other, an employer would be well advised to view reported behavior through the perspective of a reasonable person of the same gender as the employee making the complaint. In addition, the EEOC continues to use the reasonable-victim standard when it investigates charges of harassment. Thus, for example, a male manager who sees nothing wrong with certain conduct in the workplace should, in order to protect himself and his employer, look at and deal with the behavior through the perspective of the women in the workplace if doing so would result in a different understanding and response.

Is the supervisor in the case study looking at this situation through the eyes of the person who is being made uncomfortable? It is possible that Victoria looks at the displaying of the picture differently from Mark and that it has quite a dif-

ferent effect on her than on him. He should be dealing with this situation from her perspective in order not to cause more problems for his company.

The Subjective Test   The determination of whether a term or condition of employment is changed is not just an objective one. The Supreme Court in the *Harris* case added a further requirement, noting that plaintiffs must also satisfy a subjective test: whether this particular plaintiff perceived that the conditions were altered. This means that the plaintiff, herself or himself, must have been adversely affected by the behavior.

Although this may seem to add to the plaintiff's burden, the courts have in fact always had to determine that damage has occurred, and without some subjective perception, it is unlikely that a person could prove damage. Leaving an employer because of a hostile environment is unlikely if an individual does not perceive that environment to be abusive. In addition, pain and suffering damages would be difficult if not impossible to prove when there is no perception that this is the type of environment that would cause emotional damages. Thus, whereas the courts will continue to be required to find a subjective element, it is unlikely that this will have much impact on cases in this area.

In fact, in a recent case, an appeals court disagreed with the district court's determination that the plaintiff had not perceived her environment to be discriminatory because she did not consult a physician for any psychological problems, quit, avoid the office, or react angrily, and was not hindered from performing her assigned tasks. The appeals court noted that the employee had stated that the conduct upset and embarrassed her and made her feel uncomfortable, and surmised that a desire to keep her job may have been the reason for the lack of response. The employee had also complained when it was explained to her that she had some recourse and the "absence of a noticeable decline in job productivity should therefore not be unduly emphasized."[23]

Is the Behavior Unwelcome?   It is good business practice to take any potentially demeaning or sexual behavior in the workplace seriously and assume that it at least contributes to changing the terms or conditions of employment. For an employer, a more helpful determination than deciding whether an incident is serious enough to alter the condition of employment is finding out whether the behavior was "welcomed" by the employee or employees. This in fact is the gravamen or the crux of a sexual harassment case, according to the Supreme Court in *Vinson*. Any *unwelcome* behavior is potentially problematic for managers and employers. Thus, the "welcome or unwelcome" element is key in deciding on an appropriate response to the situation.

The Supreme Court in the *Vinson* case stated that conduct could be unwelcome even though it may seem to be voluntarily accepted. An employee may go along with the behavior (in fact Mechelle Vinson had intercourse with her supervisor forty or fifty times) without protest, yet if she felt she had no choice, it could still be unwelcome. This is much like the situation of a rape committed with a threat of violence. Even though the victim does not fight the rape, it cannot be said that she wanted it to occur or that, given a choice, she would have let it happen. In reality, Mechelle Vinson had no meaningful choice.

The burden of determining whether the conduct is unwelcome is not very cumbersome when the behavior is overtly belittling or demeaning. Most courts recognize that, without some overwhelming evidence, it is appropriate to presume that a harassed employee did not want to be treated in such a manner. A determination of whether the behavior is welcome appears to be more complex in the situation where the harassment takes the form of more covert behavior, including sexual propositions or other sexual behavior in the workplace. This is where asking someone for a date and sexual harassment can be differentiated. If the person welcomed the overtures, they are appropriate behavior. If not, then such behavior crosses the line into potentially costly conduct.

Admittedly, it is not inappropriate for employees to be considering a personal relationship with co-workers. When two employees are at about the same level in the organizational hierarchy, a polite and socially acceptable overture for a date or lunch would not be considered legal sexual harassment. Once the invitee has indicated no interest, however, further conduct, having been shown to be unwelcome, would then become harassment and could create, in itself or in cumulation (depending on the severity, intensity, and other factors), a discriminatory work environment.

There are times when an employee is in fact having a consensual relationship with another employee and may welcome sexual behavior from that person. As should be obvious, this does not mean that he or she can be said to welcome sexual behavior from others in the workplace. In addition, at times when a consensual relationship is ended by one of two people involved, further overtures would not be welcome. Whereas employees maintain the right to claim that behavior that was once welcome is no longer so, EEOC policies require in this situation that the employee make clear to the other partner that the relationship has concluded and further exchanges of a personal nature are not wanted.

Manifestations of unwelcomeness are not always required, however. This is especially true when a supervisor is involved in behavior with a subordinate. Because of the power differential, an employee is often not required by the courts to express disinterest before claiming that any conduct was not welcomed by her or him when the person involved in the harassment is a superior. The power differential may mean that, even though there may have been the appearance of voluntary acceptance of the behavior, it was not welcome.

Supervisors hold a tacit threat of possible retribution over employees, and even though most people would like to believe that others are interested in us for our personality and good looks, there is no way to know whether it is the threat or the natural charisma that is the reason for this situation. Some workers feel trapped into a relationship, even if the company has a mechanism in place for filing sexual harassment complaints. As one court noted, even if a channel exists for reporting such behavior, employees in some workplaces may feel that registering a complaint against a supervisor will result in more trouble than keeping quiet.

As can readily be seen, it is often not easy to determine from circumstantial evidence such as the worker's immediate response whether conduct is welcome or unwelcome. Silence, for example, in the face of an incident, like nonreporting, may not be a good indicator of welcomeness. In fact, lack of response, as one court noted, may itself be evidence of unwelcomeness. The coping mechanisms employed by some people include keeping silent and hoping that the behavior will subside. Thus, just because there is no outward sign by an employee that conduct is unwanted or that, given a choice, she or he would want this to occur, one cannot always presume otherwise.

In addition, an employee's response or behavior with regard to sexual conduct in other environments may also not be a good indicator of whether conduct is welcomed. The EEOC has stated that evidence of a party's general character and past behavior toward others has limited, if any, value in determining whether behavior is welcomed. In *Burns v. McGregor Electronic Industries,* the court agreed with the EEOC's interpretation and rejected an employer's contention that the plaintiff's own past conduct and use of foul language showed that "she was the kind of person who could not be offended by such comments and therefore welcomed them generally." The court stated that the key was whether the *particular* conduct in question was welcome and that "use of foul language or sexual innuendo in a consensual setting does not waive . . . legal protections against unwelcome harassment."[24]

In this same case, the court also pointed out the folly of making a presumption about a particular worker, regardless of her or his background. The plaintiff had claimed that a discriminatory work environment existed because nude magazine pictures of her had been posted in the workplace. The employer tried to use the fact that she had posed for such pictures as proof that she welcomed sexual behavior by her co-workers and, at the district court level, the company won on this argument. The appeals court did not agree, however, and reversed the lower court, noting that sexuality in one context was quite different than in another. Thus, someone who wishes to maintain a professional standing in the workplace might act quite differently in that environment than in an outside setting.

In the case study, Marjorie is the one who posed for the picture. Is that relevant to a determination of whether she welcomed the conduct? How about the fact that she did not want to complain? Many courts would not allow an employer to presume that the conduct was welcome, and a separate determination should be made.

An employer should also be careful not to assume that so-called un-ladylike behavior means that the employee welcomes offensive or sexual conduct. As one court noted in responding to a claim that the plaintiff's own demeanor precipitated the worker's behavior:

> Even if we ignore the question why "unladylike" behavior should provoke not a vulgar response but a hostile, harassing response, and even if [the employee's] testimony that she talked and acted as she did in an effort to be "one of the boys" is (despite its plausibility) discounted, her words and conduct cannot be compared to those of the men and used to justify their conduct and exonerate their employer. The asymmetry of positions must be considered. She was one woman; they were many men . . . Her use of terms . . . could not be deeply threatening, or her placing a hand on the thigh of one of her macho coworkers intimidating . . . We have trouble *imagining* a situation in which male factory workers sexually harass a lone woman *in self defense* as it were; yet that at root is General Motors' characterization of what happened here. It is incredible on the admitted facts.[25]

Employers would be well advised to presume any potential harassment, witnessed or reported, is unwelcome, unless there is a substantial amount of evidence that it was not. What kind of evidence could be deemed credible? This is a very tricky area. The Supreme Court has stated that evidence of the plaintiff's dress, speech, or participation in the conduct is not irrelevant, but many courts are somewhat reticent to allow the use of such evidence. For example, should the fact that a woman wears sexy clothes to work mean that she wants to be demeaned? Logically, that may be difficult to substantiate and such so-called defenses appear akin to the now discredited "she was raped because she dressed like she was asking for it" rationale. If sexy dress is occurring in a workplace, it may in fact signal that there is some belief on the part of some people that they are judged and evaluated better in that workplace when they dress and act in a sexual manner. Such a situation may raise a danger flag because it could mean that a discriminatory work environment has already been created and needs to be diffused.

> *Marjorie's mode of dress in the case study appears to signal to Mark that she is asking for the behavior that occurs. Although the Supreme Court has stated that evidence of this type would not be irrelevant in a lawsuit, few courts allow such evidence. Relying on this in any future legal action to defend against a hostile or discriminatory work environment claim would probably be foolish. Mark should focus instead on whether the behavior was indeed welcomed by Victoria—and most of the more relevant evidence would indicate otherwise.*

Courts are beginning to realize that women in particular find it difficult to respond to harassment in a manner that might overtly manifest unwelcomeness. This is especially true with regard to reporting of harassing behavior.

Many companies make the mistake of claiming that they have no harassment because none has been reported, when in fact the environment is so bad that harassed employees fear coming forward as much as enduring the problem.

There are many reasons why people hesitate to report incidents of sexual harassment, including their concerns about not being believed and the fear of publicity or being branded a troublemaker or worse. In many workplaces, these fears are well grounded as the situation does become worse if harassment is reported. These environments are usually ones in which the subject of harassment is not taken seriously, the policies and procedures are not adequate, and consequently the potential for legal liability is high. Encouraging reporting is vital, but even if no reports are forthcoming, an employer should not just assume all is well. Thus, unless a business is sure that its policy and procedures are fail-safe and ironclad (concepts that will be discussed in chapter 4), the business should not assume that courts will accept nonreporting as a manifestation that behavior was welcome.

Because nonreporting by affected employees is not always a good defense, employers may wish to encourage, or even require, reports of witnessed behavior by third parties. Managers can then sensitively inquire as to the welcomeness whenever a situation occurs. However, even if the conduct was welcomed by the person to whom the behavior is directed, it may not be legally advisable to allow it to continue. This is because courts are beginning to accept discriminatory work environment lawsuits from persons who are not themselves the focus of harassing behavior or conduct, but who are forced to work in a place where this occurs. Thus, courts are saying that those who work in an environment where demeaning, belittling, or sexual behavior is directed at other workers may also be working in a hostile or intimidating work environment and are potential plaintiffs. Allowing reports of behavior by anyone who witnesses it makes good sense managerially and legally. The person making the third-party report may be saying that this type of behavior is unwelcomed by her or him, even if the employee on whom the conduct was focused claims otherwise. This should be taken seriously and dealt with appropriately.

In the case study, Marjorie could be seen as the focus of the behavior, but Victoria is obviously bothered by it. Even if Marjorie was determined to welcome the display, it may be contributing to a hostile or discriminatory work environment for Victoria.

Examples of Harassing Behavior   A closer look at exactly what types of behavior may have the effect of creating a hostile or discriminatory work environment will help in more completely understanding this somewhat complex area. The problem with any such exploration, however, is that these types of cases are all different and very fact-specific. Thus any discussion of behavior that does create a discriminatory environment must begin from the presumption that the fact that a behavior does not fit in with previous lists does *not* mean that it is appropriate or legally defensible.

The EEOC definition of sexual harassment is intentionally vague, and the commission has made it clear that its determination of whether certain conduct creates a discriminatory environment will only be made by looking at the totality of the circumstances. Factors such as the nature of the behavior and its context can often be key.

The EEOC specifically lists "sexual advances, requests for sexual favors, and other verbal or physical conduct of a sexual nature" as possibly harassing behavior in the workplace, if they are unwelcomed by the person to whom this behavior is directed. The EEOC also views any gender-based verbal or physical conduct, even if not sexual in nature, as problematic. Inflammatory and patently offensive epithets and slurs or comments demeaning another because of his or her gender and any physical touching of intimate areas of the body can be the basis of a legal claim. In fact, the EEOC has stated that it will "presume that the unwelcome, intentional touching of a charging party's [the person making the claim of discrimination] intimate body areas is sufficiently offensive to alter the conditions of her working environment and constitute a violation of Title VII." The EEOC has also specifically noted that sexual slurs and displays of girlie pictures will be viewed as offensive.

> *Thus, the picture in the workplace in the case study has specifically been listed by the EEOC as behavior that could create a hostile environment. The company should react quickly to remove the picture.*

As will be discussed further in chapter 3, harassing behavior has been said to run on a continuum from staring at or commenting upon a woman's body all the way to conduct that can best be described as rape. This continuum can encompass a variety of conduct that may not at first glance appear to be problematic. In one case, for example, a woman manager claimed that her employer had contributed to the discriminatory or hostile work environment by requiring her to sit with the other women during a meeting, even though the other women all held subordinate positions in the company and the male managers were placed together behind the females.

In this rapidly expanding area, there appear to be some trends with regard to new problem areas for employers. Plaintiffs are alleging, for example, that a variety of work rules, especially those involving certain dress codes, are creating discriminatory environments. In one such case, the employer ordered its female lobby attendants to wear suggestive uniforms. This resulted in whistling and rude comments by customers that, the court found, demeaned the women and their roles as professional workers. The court found that the dress code created a hostile work environment and awarded damages for the plaintiffs. This trend appears to be expanding, as even restaurants that have traditionally used sex in their marketing strategies are now finding themselves facing lawsuits.

With the expansion of the kinds of behavior that could be seen as contributing to a discriminatory work environment, employers should be concerned when imposing requirements of dress on workers. Any work rules that require women to dress or act in a way that makes them sexually attractive to customers or other workers may not be advisable from a legal perspective and should be carefully examined. Of course, cleanliness and grooming standards are appropriate, but managers imposing or enforcing such standards should analyze whether they are indeed benign standards or merely ones that reinforce a view that women should dress in a sexy, attractive, or "attracting" manner.

Technology is also contributing to the ways in which sexual harassment may occur. Cases are beginning to include claims that a discriminatory environment is being created by such behavior as sexually suggestive or demeaning electronic mail messages or pornographic software on company computers. This can be especially problematic because of the possibility for anonymity in such situations, and companies may need to explore ways to pinpoint the source and handle such offensive behavior.

Another type of conduct that is sometimes the basis for sexual harassment lawsuits is favoritism. This involves a situation where the employer is sued because a supervisor bestowed favorable treatment on a person with whom she or he had a sexual relationship, and a third party claims either that she or he would have received the benefits had it not been for the relationship, or that the relationship created a hostile environment.

The EEOC has stated that Title VII does not prohibit preferential treatment based upon consensual romantic relationships. Whereas such treatment may be unfair, the agency claims that the treatment does not illegally discriminate because both men and women are disadvantaged for reasons other than their gender.

While favoritism may not be specifically deemed by the EEOC as illegal, it must be noted that at least one court has also stated that a workplace in which "affairs" are rampant may have a discriminatory effect on those forced to work in that environment. In *Broderick v. Ruder*,[26] the court noted that conduct that included romantic involvements between male supervisors and female subordinates, frequent parties, and afternoon long-lunch "hours" was harassment of the other women in the workplace who did not participate in the behavior and thus did not receive the preferential treatment.

What the favoritism situation clearly illustrates is that behavior cannot always be absolutely classified as legal or illegal. At times, courts may differ on interpretation and juries can always make their own findings of facts. Employers should be more concerned with whether behavior is a problem for an employee than with whether it reaches the level of legal liability. An appropriate response to any complaint makes good business sense.

This need to respond adequately is important for a variety of reasons. What is very clear is that a business's inadequate response to behavior, whether or not the behavior itself was adequate to meet the standard of legal severity, could be used as further evidence of a hostile environment. Thus, whereas a crude joke told by co-workers might not reach the level of Title VII liability, a response to a complaint about such behavior that demeans, intimidates, or ridicules the person making the complaint may, when added to the joke, contribute to the behavior reaching a level that the law would recognize as altering the conditions of employment. The necessity for appropriate responses by managers to each and every unwelcome harassing behavior becomes very clear. What is said and done during the course of an investigation may make the difference between a resolved problem and a time- and resource-consuming legal battle.

Clearly it is vital that managers deal with problems appropriately, not only because of an inappropriate response's potential for escalating the previous behavior to a level of legal harassment, but also because some responses may be illegal in themselves. Chapter 4 will deal more specifically with the correct handling of complaints. When potential sexual harassment is reported, managers should be very careful not to do anything that could be viewed as retaliation against an employee for making a complaint about sexual harassment. Retaliation is specifically listed as conduct that violates Title VII in the law itself, and thus an unthinking response by a manager, such as moving a complaining employee, can become extraordinarily burdensome for both the manager and the business. In addition, the law states that anyone exercising rights under Title VII is protected from retaliation, and this means that others, such as those who are witnesses or who speak up for other employees, have legal rights. Employers must be careful when making an adverse employment decision about anyone involved in a sexual harassment complaint if there is any chance that the decision may be viewed as retaliation.

Alleged Defenses   Employers in a variety of cases have tried to use affirmative defenses when they find that they have maintained a hostile or discriminatory work environment. The defenses fall into three basic categories, none of which has worked to any great degree in the courts. A business that attempts to use them should be aware of the problems.

EEO Harassers   There are circumstances when an employer may believe it can claim that there is no violation of Title VII, even though the workplace is not conducive to success. This would be a situation, for example, where a supervisor is abrasive, annoying, and downright difficult to work with no matter what the employee's gender. Although "equal opportunity harassers" do exist, a company that wishes to use this as a defense obviously does not comprehend fundamental and rudimentary human relations concepts, an obvious employee problem on its own. In addition, the fact that behavior is universal may not be a defense if the effect is seen as different on one gender than on the other. This was the result in a 1994 case involving harassment by a person the employer claimed "consistently abused men and women alike." In *Steiner v. Showboat Operating Co.,*[27] the United States Court of Appeals for the Ninth Circuit did not agree that this meant there was no discrimination for two reasons:

> The numerous depositions of Showboat employees reveal that Trenkle was indeed abusive to men, but that his abuse of women was different. It relied on sexual epithets, offensive, explicit references to women's bodies and sexual conduct. . . . [W]hile his abuse of men in no way related to their gender, his abuse of female employees, especially Steiner, centered on the fact that they were females. It is one thing to call a woman "worthless" and another to call her a "worthless broad."
>
> Furthermore, even if Trenkle used sexual epithets equal in intensity and in an equally degrading manner against male employees, he cannot thereby "cure" his conduct toward women.[28]

Thus, it may well be that the "equal opportunity harasser" defense may not be adequate to remove liability.

The Social Context Defenses Claims have been made by some employers that workers could not claim to feel threatened or demeaned by pornographic material or belittling sexual behavior because it is so prevalent in the society and also because many women view pornography themselves. As previously noted in the context of a plaintiff's social and work demeanor, the courts differentiate between what occurs in the workplace and in the outside world. When the effect of pornography on a *work* environment is understood, the context is important. Most courts reject this defense and note that Title VII is designed to change the workplace, not the whole society. This distinction is clearly explained by the following passage from a law review article often quoted by judges:

> [W]hile publicly disseminated pornography may influence all viewers, it remains the expression of the editors of *Penthouse* or *Hustler* or the directors of *Deep Throat.* On the wall of an office, it becomes the expression of a coworker or supervisor as well.
>
> In this context the effect of pornography on workplace equality is obvious. Pornography on an employer's wall or desk communicates a message about the way he views women, a view strikingly at odds with the way women wish to be viewed in the workplace. Depending upon the material in question it may communicate that women should be the objects of sexual aggression, that they are submissive slaves to male desires, or that their most salient and desirable attributes are sexual. Any of these images may communicate to male coworkers that it is acceptable to view women in a predominately sexual way. All of the views to some extent detract from the image most women in the workplace would like to project: that of the professional, credible coworker.[29]

ode◦pon

Title VII guarantees equal opportunity in employment, not on the street corners, and the attempted use of such a defense is not sound. Workers need to understand that behavior that is acceptable in their own social setting or circles may not be acceptable or allowed in the workplace.

The Status Quo Defense   Some employers have tried to show that, because the plaintiff knew the environment was discriminatory when they applied for a position, they should be required to accept a situation into which they voluntarily thrust themselves. This is a sort of an "assumption of the risk" defense, which makes the incorrect assumption that equal employment opportunity merely means equal access to employment. Title VII, as courts have concluded, requires true equal opportunity. Sometimes this requires that the old way of doing things, which is detrimental to others' best efforts, must be changed so that both genders have an even chance for success. Courts have little use for this type of claim because Title VII was designed to change discriminatory behavior, and most believe that it is the employer's duty to make sure that this happens:

> No reasonable person could imagine that General Motors was genuinely helpless, that it did all it reasonably could have done. The evidence is plain that it (or at least its gas turbine division) was unprepared to deal with problems of sexual harassment even when those problems were rubbed in its face, and also incapable of improvising a solution. Its efforts at investigation were lackluster, its disciplinary efforts nonexistent, its remedial efforts perfunctory. The U.S. Navy has been able to integrate women into the crews of warships; General Motors should have been able to integrate one woman into a tinsmith shop.[30]

The Limits of Liability for Hostile Environments   Businesses' liability for sexual harassment is very far-reaching in every jurisdiction. As employers, companies are liable under Title VII, and most state laws for the actions of supervisors and co-employees and could face both statutory and common-law claims. With regard to *quid pro quo* harassment, as discussed earlier, the standard is strict liability: if harassment happens, the employer is liable. Hostile environment liability is somewhat different. There are two different standards, depending on whether the discriminatory acts were perpetrated by a co-worker, or an "agent" or supervisor.

According to most courts, when only co-workers, clients, or customers are involved in perpetrating the conduct, liability attaches when the employer knew or should have known and did not adequately remedy the situation. An employer is deemed to know when any of its agents, usually a manager, knows about the behavior, either because of a complaint or because he or she witnessed or was told of the incident. Legally speaking, an employer "should have known" when harassing behavior is so pervasive that a reasonable employer, through its agents, should not have been able to ignore the behavior's existence. A good manager will make it his or her job to find out what is going on in the workplace and how subordinate managers are conducting themselves. If there is no earlier notice, the employer certainly is deemed to have notice when it is notified that a complaint has been filed by a government agency.

What is obvious about the direction of the courts is that anyone may potentially be seen as contributing to or creating a discriminatory work environment for employees, and thus businesspeople need to deal with behavior no matter who is involved. The law requires businesses to deal not just with the conduct of co-workers or supervisors. In addition, customers or clients who are harassing employees of a company can also create legal liability for the employer of the person being harassed. The usual cases that deal with this type of harassment involve customers harassing waitresses, but recent cases seem to be moving toward other customer or client situations. Sales staff increasingly are reporting harassing behavior by employees at client companies. Whereas these situations present a challenge with regard to the appropriate manner for handling the problem, it is clear that the fact that a company needs the goodwill of the client will not serve as a defense to a sexual harassment claim. An appropriate response in such situations might involve talking to a high-level person at the client company in a spirit of cooperative effort to solve the problem. It would not hurt to remind clients that an adequate solution would also help to reduce their potential for liability. As we will discuss later, harassers rarely target only one person and may be causing legal problems within their own company.

Liability of an employer for a supervisor's sexual harassment is even more extensive than for co-workers'. There is no notice requirement, and the Supreme Court in *Vinson* told the courts to "look to agency principles" to determine the extent of liability. Although agency principles can be rather confusing and complex, it is reasonably clear that an employer is liable for the conduct when the supervisor is acting as its agent or in an agency capacity. A short discussion of the law of agency is helpful.

A *principal,* defined by *Black's Law Dictionary* as "one who has permitted or directed another to act for his benefit and subject to his direction and control," is liable for the acts of her or his agents in various circumstances. The *Restatement of Agency,* a series of volumes that discuss common-law rules, is usually used by courts to help determine the parameters of a principal's liability for an agent's behavior.

The *Restatement* states first that any wrongdoing of the agent while the agent is operating under the actual authority of the principal is imputed back to the principal. An agent is acting under actual authority when he or she is involved either in carrying out the express authority given to the agent by the principal or in activities that are necessary in order to accomplish the express authority. When a supervisor is involved in sexual harassment, it can easily be found that this wrongdoing, which is like a common-law tort or civil wrong, is occurring while the supervisor is involved in the actual authority granted to him or her by the employer, that is, managing and controlling the workplace and the work environment.

There are courts, however, that will not impute liability if the agent is involved in intentional wrongful acts while carrying out the principal's actual authority. In that situation, there are alternate bases provided in the *Restatement* for imputing liability to the principal. These include situations where it is decided that the agent is acting under the apparent authority of the principal when the wrongdoing occurs or when the agent is aided in carrying out the wrongful act by the authority granted to him or her. Thus, a finding that the employer misled the employees into believing that the supervisor had the authority to manage the workplace in any manner, and by his or her own standards, would create apparent authority to harass. An employer can create this impression when there is no adequate policy and procedure in effect that allows alternate reporting outside of the chain of command. Moreover, if the court finds that the authority granted by the employer to control and manage the workplace has aided the supervisor in harassing the employees, this finding would also result in imputed liability.

With these many alternate bases for liability, most courts have been very consistent in making the employer liable when the supervisor is involved in the harassment. What this means, then, is that whenever and wherever the supervisor is involved with subordinate employees, any discriminatory behavior that is perpetrated by the supervisor is most likely the legal responsibility of the employer. This responsibility for the acts of a person in a supervisory capacity is imposed because the supervisor is in a position of disparate power over the employees, and the employer is required by the law to be very careful with regard to choosing those in whom it will vest such authority.

An important qualifier of this authority occurs, however, when the employer makes very clear to the employees that sexual harassment is not condoned, approved, or authorized in that workplace. A serious pronouncement and responsive action by the employer can be said to remove the apparent authority to control the work environment in a negative manner and would take away the aid to the harassment that might be afforded by unlimited power and authority. The employees must know that no one, at any level, has the right or authority to harass or create a discriminatory environment and that actions will be immediately taken upon any violation of this rule. This is done with a policy and procedures that meet the standards set out by the courts and the EEOC. Once such a policy and procedures are in place, employer liability is greatly reduced and most situations should be quickly resolved internally.

An important point to note in the area of legal liability for sexual harassment is that there may be many possible defendants in a Title VII lawsuit. While the act specifies that an employer, a labor organization, or an employment agency is liable, the definition given includes any agent of those listed. The courts are divided on the individual liability of the agents (i.e., supervisors and managers) who either perpetrated, condoned, or did not correctly handle discriminatory behavior.

The liability of the agents themselves is a new and developing area of the law. Some courts adhere to the rule that only the employer can be liable for creating a hostile environment. This means that even if a supervisor helped to create the hostile environment, he or she could not be sued individually under Title VII. There does appear to be some liability, however, for highly placed corporate managers. In the *Robinson v. Jacksonville Shipyards* case, for example, the court declared that the principles of employer liability could be broadened to include certain individual corporate officers. Noting that it is inconceivable that Congress intended to exclude from liability the very persons who have engaged in the employment practices that are the subject of the lawsuits, the court went on to declare that Title VII "works to hold responsible those who control the aspects of employment accorded protection by that law."[31]

Who are these people who could be said to exercise effective control in the workplace and make or contribute meaningfully to employment decisions? While this trend toward more extensive liability is new and developing, a look at the two individuals found liable, along with the employer, in the *Robinson* case is helpful in determining who may be personally liable under Title VII. The vice president for operations at Jacksonville Shipyards, Inc., (JSI) was found liable for the hostile work environment because "his responsibility extended to the creation and implementation of JSI's sexual harassment policies. Their failure is his failure. Additionally, he personally intervened in Robinson's complaint and directed that no remedial action be taken."[32] The Industrial Relations Manager of JSI was liable because "he held responsibility for the day-to-day administration of the sexual harassment complaint machinery. Its failure is his failure."[33] Additionally, he had also personally intervened and directed that no remedial action be taken.

Title VII does not provide for personally suing a co-worker for a violation of the act. The various common-law suits mentioned in chapter 1 are available for personally holding co-workers liable, however, and are often joined with a Title VII case. The same situation exists with regard to supervisors or managers who in some way contributed to the plaintiff's damages, even if the court does not allow a direct Title VII case against them. Thus, for example, a manager or co-worker may be sued for intentional infliction of emotional distress at the same time that the employer is sued for a violation of the federal law. The damages assessed with regard to these claims may even be higher because state common-law lawsuits, even in states with damage caps, usually allow for larger sums than does the federal statute.

Who Can File a Harassment Claim?

Anyone in the workplace could potentially find herself or himself facing some form of sexual harassment. Women and men are both protected by Title VII. If a man is subjected to sexual harassment, he has a claim, just as does a woman.

> *Mark Steel in the case study may file a claim under Title VII if he believes that he has been subjected to sexual harassment by his supervisor. Men and women have the right to equal employment opportunity.*

An employee may file a harassment claim when she or he has been harassed by someone in authority or by those who are equal in organizational power. There are also some new lawsuits in the area of sexual harassment that involve lawsuits by supervisors who have been harassed by subordinates. Although such situations may be hard to imagine because of the power that supervisors hold over subordinates, psychologists have identified the fact that there are many sources of power in the workplace. One of these is gender power, which may allow some workers to feel more comfortable and safe being involved in behavior or conduct which demeans a woman who is higher in the organizational chain of command. If this is coupled with a lack of support in the company for tough disciplinary measures by the female supervisor, a hostile environment might be legally sustainable. Although it is not clear what the limits of this would be, it is advisable for companies to make it clear, by word and action, that they stand strongly behind their female managers in trying to control these types of problems. This requires helping to enforce training and disciplinary decisions at all levels of the organization and making sure that others in the managerial ranks are not doing or saying anything that might undermine the authority of the supervisor involved in the problematic situation. Any behavior or conduct directed at a supervisor that would fit under the usual hostile environment parameters should be viewed as seriously as the company views other insubordination.

Damages Available
in Sexual Harassment Lawsuits

When employees are able to prove that legal sexual harassment has occurred, there are a variety of damages that they can receive. Some of these can add up to hundreds of thousands and even millions of dollars.

EQUITABLE DAMAGES

Title VII allows a judge or jury to award what are termed *equitable* damages. These include back pay for a period not to exceed two years; attorney's fees; reinstatement to the position that the employee would have been in and seniority to which the employee would have been entitled had the discrimination not occurred; orders to cease and desist the harassing conduct; injunctions against further harassment or injunctions that require the employer to create a comprehensive sexual harassment policy and procedures; and occasionally front pay that is granted for a period of time to allow the employee to recover from the emotional effects of harassment and begin new employment.

Back pay is usually available to an employee who is discharged from a company for a discriminatory reason. When an employee quits the company of his or her own volition and files a lawsuit, employers have challenged an award of back pay on the basis that this remedy is not available to those who leave employment voluntarily. Although this has traditionally been true, the courts have usually tempered this by applying the doctrine of *constructive discharge.* In most jurisdictions, an employee can be found to have been constructively discharged if the court or jury determines (1) that the environment was so abusive that a reasonable employee would have felt compelled to resign and (2) that the resignation was actually caused by the harassment. In a few circuits, there is also a requirement that the employer intended to cause the resignation of the harassed employee. Whereas this could be a difficult thing for plaintiffs to prove, some courts that require this element have modified it somewhat, often allowing a conclusion of intent based on the fact that a person is held to intend the foreseeable consequences of his or her conduct. Thus, if the conduct is unreasonably abusive, the resignation of the victim could be a foreseeable consequence.

As stated previously, back pay is awarded where an employee has been removed from the job for a discriminatory reason. Sometimes, however, even though a nondiscriminatory reason is the basis of the discharge, back pay may also be available if that reason can be tied to the harassment.

Employers often contend, for example, that they discharged a worker for excessive absences and thus that back pay should not be available. In some cases, however, courts have found that the absences themselves were caused by the abusive environment and still will award back pay. This has also occurred in situations where the employer claimed that the reason for the discharge was a poor work attitude, insubordination, or a deterioration in job performance, if the court determined that such behavior was the result of the discriminatory work environment. As one court noted:

> [A]n expert on sexual harassment on the job . . . testified that women subject to sexual harassment will have increases in work performance problems, including increases in on the job errors, as a direct result of harassment on the job.[34]

This correlation between deteriorated job performance and other work-quality problems and harassment is an important one for businesses to keep in mind. Although it may seem that there is a perfectly acceptable reason to fire an employee who is not doing an adequate job, it is often necessary to do a more complete investigation of the situation. This may mean discussing the situation in a nonthreatening environment with the employee to make sure that there is no discriminatory situation looming in the background. If so, taking care of the problem with regard to the environment should also take care of the problem of the inadequate worker performance, without the potential future liability.

OTHER DAMAGES

Although it originally allowed only equitable damages, the federal law was changed in 1991 to allow pain and suffering damages in cases of intentional discrimination. In addition, punitive damages are now allowed in situations where the employer acted with malice or with reckless indifference to the rights of the plaintiff. Both kinds of damages have been awarded in sexual harassment cases. These compensatory damages are capped, however, on a sliding scale depending on the size of the company. This sliding scale allows up to $50,000 for businesses with 15–100 employees; up to $100,000 for 101–200 employees; up to $200,000 for 201–500 employees; and up to $300,000 for more than 500 employees. Under common law and many state civil rights acts, these damages are also available, but there is often no cap on the pain and suffering damages. This can result in the very high jury awards that are now beginning to be seen.

Summary

The law with regard to sexual harassment, especially harassment that creates a hostile or discriminatory environment, continues to evolve and develop as new cases are heard. It is not easy to predict how far liability might extend in the future, or to come up with a comprehensive list of behaviors that will be seen as contributing to a hostile environment. All that is clear is that the best course for an employer or manager to take to avoid liability is to better understand the whole concept of sexual harassment, including its basis and its effects, and then adopt and carry out stringent sexual harassment policies and procedures. Taking the matter seriously from the beginning may remove the necessity to take it even more seriously in the courtroom in the future. It has been estimated that each day in court can cost an employer over $100,000, and that is serious business for anyone.

Clearly, there is no need for any business to find itself charged in a sexual harassment lawsuit. Liability can be avoided, but unfortunately there may always be those who do not take the prudent path. Until everyone understands and responds appropriately, the law will continue to provide a remedy for employees with no other recourse, remedies that can be very costly for the employers.

For Reflection

1. Discuss why it is so difficult to exactly define the term *sexual harassment.*
2. Differentiate between *quid pro quo* and hostile environment lawsuits.
3. Explain why a lack of reporting does not necessarily indicate that there is no problem in the workplace.
4. Discuss the reasonable woman standard. To what does it apply? Why do courts use it?
5. Explain why courts and the EEOC differentiate between a person's social and workplace behavior.
6. Discuss the concept of agency as it relates to employer liability for sexual harassment.
7. Why must harassing behavior affect a term or condition of employment in order to be the basis of a lawsuit?
8. When does harassing behavior affect a term or condition of employment? What definitive test can be used to make that determination?
9. Discuss why employers need to be concerned with the conduct of clients or customers.
10. What did the Supreme Court determine in the *Vinson* case? In the *Harris* case?
11. Why is *quid pro quo* so serious for employers?
12. List five actions that an employer can take to help avoid liability for sexual harassment.
13. What are EEOC guidelines?
14. What is a constructive discharge? What is its relevance in a sexual harassment lawsuit?
15. Explain why an employer may have difficulty using the "EEO harasser," "status quo," or "social context" defenses.

Notes

1. Title VII also covers labor organizations and employment agencies. Sexual harassment standards also apply to these groups, but this book, in keeping with its intent to clarify the law with regard to workplace harassment, will only use the term *employer.*
2. Barnes v. Costle, 561 F.2d 983 (D.C. Cir. 1977).
3. Karibian v. Columbia University, 14 F.3d 773 (2d Cir. 1994).
4. *Karibian* at 778.
5. Michele Galen et al., *Sexual Harassment: Out of the Shadows,* BUSINESS WEEK, October 28, 1991, at 30.
6. Meritor Savings Bank v. Vinson, 477 U.S. 57 (1986).
7. *Vinson* at 65.
8. Harris v. Forklift Systems, 114 S.Ct. 367, 371 (1993).
9. Ellison v. Brady, 924 F.2d 892 (9th Cir. 1991).
10. *Ellison* at 873.
11. *Ellison* at 875 n. 4.

12. Harris v. Forklift Systems, 114 S.Ct. 367 (1993).

13. Henson v. City of Dundee, 682 F.2d 897, 904 (11th Cir. 1982).

14. *Harris* at 370.

15. *Harris* at 371.

16. *Vinson* at 67.

17. *Harris* at 371.

18. Robinson v. Jacksonville Shipyards, 760 F. Supp. 1486, 1524 (M.D. Fla. 1991).

19. Lipsett v. University of Puerto Rico, 864 F.2d 881 (1st Cir. 1988).

20. Andrews v. City of Philadelphia, 895 F.2d 1469 (3d Cir. 1990).

21. Burns v. McGregor Electronic Industries, 989 F.2d 959 (8th Cir. 1993).

22. First stated by Judge Damon Keith in his dissent in Rabidue v. Osceola Refining, 805 F.2d 611, 626 (6th Cir. 1986).

23. Dey v. Colt Const. & Development Co., 28 F. 3d 1446 (7th Cir. 1994).

24. *Burns* at 963.

25. Carr v. Allison Gas Turbine Div., General Motors, 32 F.3d 1007, 1011 (7th Cir. 1994).

26. Broderick v. Ruder, 685 F. Supp. 1269 (D. D.C. 1994).

27. Steiner v. Showboat Co., 25 F.3d 1459 (9th Cir. 1994).

28. *Steiner* at 1464.

29. Kathryn Abrams, *Gender Discrimination and the Transformation of Workplace Norms,* 42 VANDERBILT LAW REVIEW 1183, 1212 n. 118 (1989).

30. *Carr* at 1012.

31. *Robinson* at 1527.

32. *Robinson* at 1528.

33. *Robinson* at 1528.

34. Moffett v. Gene B. Glick Co., 621 F. Supp. 244, 262 (N.D. Ind. 1985), *rev'd on other grounds,* 644 F. Supp. 983 (N.D. Ind. 1986).

CHAPTER

Sexual Harassment from the Psychological Perspective

It is only after a great deal of agonizing consideration that I am able to talk of these unpleasant matters to anyone, except my closest friends. . . . Telling the world is the most difficult experience of my life. . . . I may have used poor judgment early on in my relationship with this issue. I was aware, however, that telling at any point in my career could adversely affect my future career. . . . Perhaps I should have taken angry or even militant steps . . . but I must confess to the world that the course that I took seemed the better, as well as the easier, approach.

—Anita Hill,
Senate Judiciary Confirmation Hearings
of Clarence Thomas, 1991

I cannot imagine anything that I said or did to Anita Hill that could have been mistaken for sexual harassment. With that said, if there is anything that I have said that has been misconstrued by Anita Hill or anyone else to be sexual harassment, then I can say that I'm so very sorry, I wish I had known; if I did know I would have stopped immediately. . . .

—Clarence Thomas,
Senate Judiciary Confirmation Hearings
of Clarence Thomas, 1991

45

CASE STUDY

Mary has just arrived at her first job. Upon her arrival she is met by a supervisor who shows considerable interest in her work and experience in college. Mary is flattered by his interest and agrees to discuss her ideas related to her work over lunch in a restaurant downtown. After a few lunches where the conversation is general and social rather than focused on professional issues, Mary finds that he is touching her—rubbing his knees against hers, placing his hand on her back and arms, and once patting her on the bottom. He asks Mary to meet him outside of work for early dinners. She declines, offering various excuses, and tries to maintain a polite but distant tone in her conversations with him. One day he asks Mary to come into his office to discuss a project. Once she is inside the office, he closes the door, moves toward her, and puts his arms around her. Mary tries to push him away, but he holds her tighter and tries to kiss her. There is a knock on the door, he releases Mary, and she opens the door and hurries out of the office.

Is this sexual harassment? Why or why not? If you believe this is sexual harassment, when did the harassment begin?

Introduction

How did you answer the questions in the case study? Do you believe sexual harassment occurred between the supervisor and new employee? Most individuals to whom this scenario is shown agree that sexual harassment occurred. However, answers to the second question (When did the harassment begin?) are typically quite different. For example, most women report the harassment began when the supervisor started to ask Mary out for lunch; most men, on the other hand, believe the sexual harassment began when the supervisor cornered Mary in his office. When do you believe the sexual harassment began?

The responses to this scenario, adapted from Paludi and Barickman,[1] illustrate how much confusion still exists because of a lack of a clear, concise, and widely accepted definition of sexual harassment. Definitions of sexual harassment are important because they educate individuals in the workplace and promote discussion and conscientious evaluation of experiences.

There are two major types of definitions of sexual harassment. The first type includes legal and regulatory constructions. We addressed the first type of definition in chapter 2. The second type of definition is developed empirically by investigating what various groups of individuals perceive sexual harassment to be under different circumstances. This chapter will focus on the second type of definition, based on actual behaviors that constitute sexual harassment. Following an overview of the definitions, we will discuss the differential interpretations that women and men in the workplace give to these behaviors. We will also address the relationship between the way individuals define sexual harassment and how they cope with this form of victimization.

Empirical Definition of Sexual Harassment

Empirical definitions of sexual harassment are data based and most generally developed by researchers in the field of human-resource management and psychology. Empirical definitions are derived from women's and men's descriptions of their experiences of harassment. These descriptions are categorized, and the categories are then used as the elements of the definition. For example, Frank Till[2] classified the responses to an open-ended sexual harassment survey of college women and derived the following five categories of generally increasing severity:

gender harassment
seductive behavior
sexual bribery
sexual coercion
sexual imposition or assault

According to Till's research, *gender harassment* consists of generalized sexist remarks and behavior not designed to elicit sexual cooperation but rather to convey insulting, degrading, or sexist attitudes about women. *Seductive behavior* is unwanted, inappropriate, and offensive sexual advances. *Sexual bribery* is the solicitation of sexual activity or other sex-linked behavior by promise of a reward (e.g., salary increase or promotion). *Sexual coercion* is the solicitation of sexual activity by threat of punishment (e.g., failure to give a promotion or being fired), and *sexual imposition or assault* includes gross sexual imposition, assault, and rape.

> *In the case study, Mary experienced* seductive behavior *on the part of her supervisor when he touched her, rubbed his knees against hers, and invited her to dinners. She experienced* sexual imposition *in her supervisor's office when he held her tightly and attempted to kiss her.*

The legal definition identifies the conditions under which a behavior may constitute sexual harassment, but generally does not give specific examples. Empirical definitions rely on the responses of individuals asked to describe their experiences. These definitions are limited to the data provided by a particular sample. Several researchers have attempted to bridge the benefits of both types of definitions. For example, Louise Fitzgerald and Alayne Omerod suggested that a definition of sexual harassment should identify that sexual harassment: (1) is the sexualization of a professional relationship; (2) frequently occurs in the context of an organizational power differential (e.g., supervisor-employee); (3) can occur in the absence of a formal power differential (e.g., hostile environment); (4) consists of unwanted and unwelcome behaviors—both verbal and nonverbal in nature; and (5) can be viewed along a continuum, from sexist remarks to nonverbal seductive gestures to sexual assault.[3]

This type of definition includes both the legal description of the nature and elements of sexual harassment and an enumeration of types of harassment based on an empirically derived classification scheme. This definition also addresses contextual issues by assuming that all sexist or sexual behaviors constitute harassment when they occur within the framework of a formal power differential. When the participants are of equal formal power, it is the recipient's reactions that constitute the defining factor.

Now that we have presented the legal and psychological interpretations of sexual harassment, it is time to summarize this information.

1. Sexual harassment does not fall within the range of personal private relationships. Harassment happens when a person with power abuses that power to intimidate, coerce, or humiliate someone because of her or his sex.

2. Verbal harassment may include unwelcomed

   sexual innuendos, comments and sexual remarks

   suggestive, obscene, or insulting sounds

   implied or overt threats

   pressure for sex

3. Physical harassment may include unwelcomed

   patting, pinching, or brushing up against the body

   coerced sexual intercourse

   assault

   leering or ogling

   obscene gestures

4. Sexual harassment is a breach of the trust that normally exists among employees.

5. Sexual harassment does create confusion because the boundary between professional roles and personal relationships is blurred. The harasser introduces a sexual element into what should be a professional situation.

6. Sexual harassment can be an action that occurs only once, or it may be repeated.

7. In voluntary sexual relationships, individuals can exercise freedom of choice in deciding whether to establish a close, intimate relationship. This freedom of choice is absent in sexual harassment.

These answers to the question "What is sexual harassment?" are crucial to the process of helping those who have been sexually harassed because most victims do not know the definition. Consequently they do not identify what has happened to them as sexual harassment. The incidence of sexual harassment thus reflect an underreporting of this abuse.

In exhibit 3.1 we list some additional case studies for you to review.

EXHIBIT 3.1

Sample Case Studies on Sexual Harassment

Do you think sexual harassment occurred in each of the following scenarios? Why or why not?

Jamie's boss insists that the waitresses wear short black skirts and low-cut white blouses to work at the café. Jamie asks her boss if this dress code has to be put into effect because she feels very uncomfortable in this outfit: customers ogle her and comment about her breast size and buttocks. Jamie's boss reminds her that he can find someone to replace her very quickly.

Danielle's co-workers have been using their electronic-mail system to rate Danielle and other women employees in terms of their sexual attractiveness. Lately Danielle hears her co-workers snicker as she goes by their desks. She has decided to take some of her vacation days in hopes that this behavior will cease by the time she returns to work.

Pat's supervisor has asked Pat out for drinks and dinner for the last few weeks. Pat has refused the supervisor's requests. Pat called a meeting to discuss receiving a fairly negative three-month performance appraisal. In this meeting, the supervisor says, "You had your chance."

Don has been visiting Antoinette at her desk in the front office, and both have started to engage in sexual banter. They also touch each other and engage in "cat calls" right in front of the other secretaries. Dru, a secretary whose desk is right next to Antoinette's, feels uneasy about the banter and touching. She doesn't find the jokes funny—in fact, she thinks they're sexist. She wishes she could have her desk moved because she can't seem to concentrate on her work whenever Don and Antoinette are together.

Incidence of Sexual Harassment in the Workplace

Sexual harassment is similar to other forms of sexual victimization such as rape, incest, and domestic violence in which various factors combine to produce underreporting and underestimates. Several major studies (as well as smaller-scale ones) do suggest that sexual harassment in the workplace is widespread. It does appear reasonable (as well as conservative) to estimate that one out of every two women will be harassed at some point in her work life. This estimate indicates that sexual harassment is the most widespread of all forms of sexual victimization studied thus far.[4] For men, as we will discuss, the incidence is substantially less.

The United States Merit Systems Protection Board addressed sexual harassment in the federal workplace and reported that 42 percent of all women employees reported being sexually harassed.[5] Merit Systems reported that many incidents occurred repeatedly, were of long duration, and had a sizable practical impact, costing the government an estimated minimum of $189 million over the two-year period covered by the research project.

Results also indicated that 33 percent of the women reported receiving unwanted sexual remarks, 28 percent reported suggestive looks, and 26 percent reported being deliberately touched. These behaviors were classified in the study as "less severe" types of sexual harassment. When "more severe" forms of sexual harassment were addressed, 15 percent of the women reported experiencing pressure for dates, 9 percent reported being directly pressured for sexual favors, and 9 percent had received unwanted letters and telephone calls. One percent of the sample had experienced actual or attempted rape or assault. Merit Systems repeated their study of workplace sexual harassment in 1987 and reported identical results to their 1981 findings.

Research by Barbara Gutek on women in the civilian workplace reports similar findings as well: approximately half the female workforce experiences sexual harassment.[6] Based on telephone interviews generated through random-digit dialing procedures, Gutek's results suggested that 53 percent of women had reported one incident they believed was sexual harassment during their working lives, including degrading, insulting comments (15 percent), sexual touching (24 percent), socializing expected as part of the job requirement (11 percent), and expected sexual activity (8 percent).

OCCUPATIONAL GROUP DIFFERENCES

Some studies reported in the literature suggest that group differences in sexual harassment are common. For example, Fitzgerald et al. found that women who were employed in a university setting (e.g., faculty, staff, and administrators) were more likely to experience sexual harassment than were women students in the same institution.[7] Gold reported that her sample of blue-collar tradeswomen experienced significantly higher levels of all forms of sexual harassment (e.g., gender harassment, seductive behavior, sexual bribery, sexual coercion, and sexual assault) than did either white-collar professional women or pink-collar clerical women.[8] LaFontaine and Tredeau also reported similar findings in their sample of 160 women, all college graduates employed in male-populated occupations (e.g., engineering and management).[9]

Nancy Baker studied a sample of one hundred women employed in either traditional or nontraditional occupations, where traditionality was defined by the sex distribution in the work group.[10] Baker also divided the traditional group into pink- and blue-collar workers. The pink-collar group comprised women who were secretaries and clerical workers. The blue-collar group comprised women who were industrial workers. Baker reported that high levels of sexual harassment are associated with having low numbers of women in the work group. For example, machinists reported significantly high frequencies of all levels of sexual harassment. Clerical women reported experiences that were more similar to those of the traditional blue-collar workers than the nontraditional blue-collar workers. Baker also reported that women in the pink-collar and traditional blue-collar groups encountered just as many men as the machinists during the workday, but were treated differently. Thus, these results suggest that as women approach numerical parity in various segments of the workforce, sexual harassment may decline.

This perspective has also been raised by Gutek, who argued that sexual harassment is more likely to occur in occupations in which "sex-role spillover" has occurred.[11] Gutek's model suggests that when occupations are dominated by one sex or the other, the sex role of the dominant sex influences (e.g., spills over) the work-role expectations for that job. Thus, sexual harassment can be viewed as a side effect of organizing society around gender stereotypes, an issue to which we now turn.

Gender Stereotyping: Relationship to Sexual Harassment

Gender stereotypes are the structured set of beliefs people hold about personal attributes of men and women, as well as their physical characteristics and behaviors.[12] Gender stereotypes are not based on factual information; they are the thoughts or cognitions we all hold about the supposed nature of women and men. For example, women are typically perceived as helpful, loyal, patient, submissive, dependent, nurturing, and sexual. Men are typically perceived as independent, dominant, and aggressive. These gender stereotypes are not left behind when women and men go to work each day. Some occupations that individuals perceive as most suitable for women are congruent with beliefs about women being nurturing, loyal, helpful, and so on (e.g., teacher, nurse). Moreover, some occupations deemed suitable for women emphasize women's status as a sex-object (e.g., cocktail waitress, flight attendant).

Gender stereotypes imply that men should be sexually aggressive and women should be ready and willing to be sex objects. Sexual harassment may occur when these gender stereotypes spill over into the workplace. Thus, when individuals act on their thoughts about women and men, they may engage in behavior that is discriminatory. For example, research suggests that women are evaluated less favorably than men for identical performance on a job.[13] In addition, men tend to turn their focus away from women and also to move away from them in contrast to their behavior toward other men.[14] Furthermore, men have higher expectations for other men's ability than for women's ability; thus, they attribute women's successful performance on the job to luck, cheating, sexuality, or the fact that someone likes them. The causal attribution of lack of ability, however, is used by men to describe anything not perfect about women's job performance. In exhibit 3.2 we present a list of some myths and realities related to women and men in the workplace.

Thus, to categorize individuals according to criteria means their suitability will be evaluated by these terms as well. In the workplace, this process produces discriminatory behavior when it leads an individual to judge or evaluate a co-worker or subordinate based on some quality unrelated to job performance. The workplace is not insulated from gender stereotyping. Women employees may be evaluated by their co-workers and supervisors in terms of their sexuality and their performance as sex objects instead of their merit as workers. Gender stereotypes are related to the amount of perceived power one has in the workplace. It is to this issue—the interrelationships between gender and power—that we now turn in our discussion of why sexual harassment occurs.

A Psychological Analysis of Why Sexual Harassment Occurs

MEN'S RELATIONSHIPS WITH MEN

Kathryn Quina related common forms of sexual harassment in the workplace to characters in the comic strip Beetle Bailey:

> General Halftrack is the archetypic older gentleman whose dowdy wife starves him for affection. His secretary, Miss Buxley—who can't type—drives him wild with her sexy figure and short skirts. "Killer" (short for "lady killer"—a curiously violent name) is always whistling at "chicks" (who love it), accompanied by Beetle, who is equally aggressive but not as successful. Zero just stares at women's bodies.[15]

EXHIBIT 3.2

Myths and Realities of Gender Comparisons

Myth: Women have lower self-esteem than men.

Fact: Overall, women and men are similar in their personal views of self-confidence and self-esteem. They do, however, differ in the areas in which they feel self-confident. Women are more likely to rate themselves as higher in social competence, whereas men see themselves as powerful and dominant.

Myth: Women lack the motivation to achieve.

Fact: Women and men can be equally motivated to achieve, but both are influenced by different factors that push their achievement levels. Women are motivated to achieve in situations where there is less competition or social comparison.

Myth: Women are more suggestible than men.

Fact: Women are just as likely as men to imitate others' behavior spontaneously. When there is pressure to conform to an ambiguous situation, women and men are equally susceptible to persuasive face-to-face communication.

Myth: Men are more analytical than women.

Fact: To analyze, one must disregard unimportant aspects of a situation in favor of the important features of a task. Both women and men are just as apt to pay attention to unimportant details as to the important ones.

Myth: Men are more affected by environment; women, by heredity.

Fact: Both men and women are affected by both heredity and environment—parents, teachers, peers, media.

From James A. Doyle and Michele A. Paludi, *Sex and Gender: The Human Experience,* 3rd edition. Copyright © 1995 Times Mirror Higher Education Group, Inc., Dubuque, Iowa. All Rights Reserved. Reprinted by permission.

Quina reminds us that although we may laugh when reading the comic strip, these scenarios are not humorous when played out in the workplace. In some new theorizing about why men sexually harass women, Paludi has focused not on men's attitudes toward women but instead on men's attitudes toward other men, competition, and power.[16] Many of the men with whom Paludi has discussed sexual harassment often act out of extreme competitiveness and concern with ego, or out of fear of losing their positions of power. They don't want to appear weak or less masculine in the eyes of other men, so they will engage in rating women's bodies, pinching women, making implied or overt threats, or spying on women. Women are the game to impress other men. When men are being encouraged to be obsessively competitive and concerned with dominance, it is likely that they will eventually use violent means to achieve dominance. Men are also likely to be abusive verbally and intimidating in their body language. Deindividuation is quite common among male office workers who, during their lunch break, rate women co-workers numerically as they walk by in the cafeteria. These men discontinue self-evaluation and adopt group norms and attitudes. Under these circumstances, group members behave more aggressively than they would as individuals.

AGGRESSION AND SEXUAL HARASSMENT

The element of aggression that is so deeply embedded in the masculine gender role is present in sexual harassment. For many men, aggression is one of the major ways of proving their masculinity, especially among those men who feel some sense of powerlessness in their lives. The theme of male-as-dominant or male-as-aggressor is so central to many men's self-concept that it literally carries over into their interpersonal communications, especially with women co-workers. Sexualizing a professional relationship may be the one way that such a man can still prove his masculinity when he can find few other ways to prove himself in control, or to be the dominant person in a relationship. Thus, sexual harassment is not so much a deviant act as an over-conforming act of the masculine gender role in this culture.

WHO HARASSES?

Harassers are found in all types of occupations, at all organizational levels, among business and professional individuals, as well as among college professors. It may be difficult for us to confront the reality that sexual harassment is perpetrated by individuals who are familiar to us and who have family lives similar to our own. Men who sexually harass have not been distinguishable from their colleagues who don't harass with respect to age, marital status, faculty rank, occupation, or academic discipline.[17] Men who harass have a tendency to do this repeatedly to many women, and men who harass hold attitudes toward women that are traditional, not egalitarian.

For example, John Pryor noted that sexual harassment bears a conceptual similarity to rape.[18] He developed a series of hypothetical scenarios that provided opportunities for sexual harassment if the man so chose. Men participating in this study were instructed to imagine themselves in the roles of the men in the scenarios and to consider what they would do in each situation. They were further instructed to imagine that, whatever their chosen course of action, no negative consequences would result from their choices. Men's scores on the survey, measuring their likelihood to engage in sexual harassment, were related to gender-role stereotyping and negatively related to feminist attitudes and that component of empathy having to do with the ability to take the standpoint of the other.

Thus, this research suggests that the man who is likely to initiate severe sexually harassing behavior appears to be one who emphasizes male social and sexual dominance, and who demonstrates insensitivity to other individuals' perspectives. Furthermore, men are less likely than women to define sexual harassment as including jokes, teasing remarks of a sexual nature, and unwanted suggestive looks or gestures. Men are also significantly more likely than women to agree with the following statements, taken from Paludi's "attitudes toward victim blame and victim responsibility" survey:

Women often claim sexual harassment to protect their reputations.

Many women claim sexual harassment if they have consented to sexual relations but have changed their minds afterwards.

Sexually experienced women are not really damaged by sexual harassment.

It would do some women good to be sexually harassed.

Women put themselves in situations in which they are likely to be sexually harassed because they have an unconscious wish to be harassed.

In most cases when a woman is sexually harassed, she deserved it.

We need to think of sexual harassment as being not the act of a disturbed man, but rather an act of an overconforming man. In other words, sexual harassment, similar to rape, incest, and battering, may be understood as an extreme acting out of qualities that are regarded as supermasculine in this culture: aggression, power, dominance, and force. Thus, men who harass are not pathological but rather exhibit behaviors characteristic of the masculine gender role in American culture.

CAN AND DO WOMEN HARASS MEN?

We can summarize the research in this area as follows:

1. Women are highly unlikely to date or initiate sexual relationships with their coworkers or supervisors.
2. A small number of men in the workplace believe they have been sexually harassed by women. The behaviors many of these men label as sexual harassment, however, do not fit the legal definition of either *quid pro quo* or hostile environment sexual harassment.
3. Men are more likely than women to interpret a particular behavior as sexual. For example, in research by Barbara Gutek, men were likely to label a business lunch as a "date" if it is with a woman manager.

4. The great majority of men report that they are flattered by women's advances, whereas women report feeling annoyed, insulted, and threatened.

5. It is rare for a woman to hold the organizational and sociocultural power that would allow her to reward a man for sexual cooperation or punish him for withholding it, even if gender-role prescriptions did not ensure that she was extremely unlikely to demand sexual favors in the first place.

Thus, although it is theoretically possible for women to harass men, in practice it is a rare event. This is due to both the women's relative lack of formal power and the socialization that stigmatizes the sexually assertive woman. Many of men's experiences with sexual harassment are with other men. Consequently, men may be reluctant to disclose this information due to homophobic concerns.

SEXUAL HARASSMENT: WOMEN, MEN, SEX, POWER, AND AGGRESSION

Sandra Tangri and her colleagues have labeled three theoretical models that incorporate this gender/power/aggression analysis.[19] The *natural/biological model* interprets sexual harassment as a consequence of sexual interactions between people, either attributing a stronger sex drive to men than to women (i.e., men "need" to engage in aggressive sexual behavior) or describing sexual harassment as part of the "game" between sexual equals. This model does not account for the extreme stress reactions suffered by victims of sexual harassment.

The *sociocultural model* posits sexual harassment as only one manifestation of the much larger patriarchal system in which men are the dominant group. Therefore, harassment is an example of men asserting their personal power based on sex. According to this model, sex would be a better predictor of both recipient and initiator status than would organizational position. Thus, women should be much more likely to be victims of sexual harassment, especially when they are in male-populated occupations. This model gives a much more accurate account of sexual harassment because the overwhelming majority of victims are women and the overwhelming majority of harassers are men.

The *organizational model* asserts that sexual harassment results from opportunities presented by relations of power and authority that derive from the hierarchical structure of organizations. Thus, sexual harassment is an issue of organizational power. Because workplaces are defined by vertical stratification and asymmetrical relations between supervisors and subordinates, individuals can use the power of their position to extort sexual gratification from their subordinates.

Related to this are the research findings that suggest that individuals who harass typically do not label their behavior as sexual harassment despite the fact they report they frequently engage in behaviors that fit the legal definition of sexual harassment. Such individuals deny the inherent power differential between themselves and their employees, as well as the psychological power conferred by this differential that is as salient as the power derived from evaluation.

The behavior that legally constitutes harassment is just that, despite what the supervisor's or co-worker's intentions may be. The impact on the individual—her or his reaction to the behavior—is the critical variable.

Interpretation of Sexual Harassment: Impact on Recipients

Several reports have documented the high cost of sexual harassment to women. Louise Fitzgerald and Alayne Ormerod noted that the outcomes of the harassment/victimization process can be examined from three main perspectives: work-related, psychological or emotional, and physiological or health-related.[20]

Work-related outcomes. In the original Merit Systems study (1981), 10 percent of the women who reported they were sexually harassed reported changing jobs as a result. In their 1987 study, Merit Systems noted that over thirty-six thousand federal employees left their jobs due to sexual harassment in the two-year period covered by the study. This number included individuals who quit, were fired, transferred, or were reassigned because of unwanted sexual attention. Additional research has documented decreased morale, absenteeism, decreased job satisfaction, performance decrements, and damage to interpersonal relationships at work.

Psychological outcomes. The consequences to women students and employees of being harassed have been devastating to their emotional health. Psychological outcomes of harassment include depression, helplessness, strong fear reactions, loss of control, disruption of victims' lives, and decreased motivation.[21] Research has indicated that, depending on the severity of the harassment, between 21 percent and 82 percent of women report that their emotional condition deteriorated as a result of the sexual harassment. Furthermore, like victims of rape who go to court, sexual harassment victims experience a second victimization when they attempt to deal with the situation through legal or institutional means. Stereotypes about sexual harassment and women's victimization blame women for the harassment. These stereotypes center around the myths that sexual harassment is a form of seduction, that women secretly want to be sexually harassed, and that women do not tell the truth.

Physiological outcomes. The following physical symptoms have been reported in the literature concerning academic and workplace sexual harassment:

headaches, sleep disturbances, disordered eating, gastrointestinal disorders, nausea, weight loss or gain, and crying spells.[22] Recently, researchers and clinicians have argued that victims of sexual harassment can exhibit a post-abuse syndrome characterized by shock, emotional numbing, constriction of affect, flashbacks, and other signs of anxiety and depression.

In recent years, the label *Sexual Harassment Trauma Syndrome* has been applied to the effects of sexual harassment on physical, emotional, interpersonal, and career aspects of employees' lives. Components of this syndrome are presented in exhibit 3.3. These responses are influenced by disappointment in the way others react and the stress of harassment-induced life changes such as moves, loss of income, and disrupted work history.

A recent study of the cost of sexual harassment by the New York Division of Human Rights documented the actual monetary costs women have experienced as a result of alleged sexual harassment, including legal expenses, medical costs, and psychotherapy costs.[23] In addition, this study also reported the number of individuals who lost health benefits, life insurance, pensions, or other benefits as a result of the alleged harassment. Furthermore, a loss or change in job status affected access to day-care arrangements.

Fitzgerald, Gold, and Brock constructed an empirically based system for classifying individuals' responses to sexually harassing behaviors.[24] They have classified individuals' responses into two categories: *internally focused strategies* and *externally focused strategies*. Internal strategies represent attempts to manage the emotions and cognitions associated with the behaviors victims have experienced. Fitzgerald et al. identified the following classification system for internally focused strategies:

Detachment
  Individual minimizes situation; treats it like a joke
Denial
  Individual denies behaviors; attempts to forget about situation
Relabeling
  Individual reappraises situation as less threatening; offers excuses for harasser's behaviors
Illusory control
  Individual attempts to take responsibility for harassment
Endurance
  Individual puts up with behavior because of not believing help is available or fearing retaliation

Externally focused strategies focus on the harassing situation itself, including reporting the behavior to the individual charged with investigating complaints of sexual harassment. Fitzgerald, Gold, and Brock classified externally focused strategies into the following categories.

EXHIBIT 3.3

Sexual Harassment Trauma Syndrome

Common Symptoms Include

CAREER EFFECTS
Changes in work habits
Drop in work performance because of stress
Absenteeism
Withdrawal from work
Changes in career goals

EMOTIONAL REACTIONS
Shock, denial
Anger, frustration
Insecurity, embarrassment
Confusion, self-consciousness
Shame, powerlessness
Guilt, isolation

PHYSICAL REACTIONS
Headaches
Inability to concentrate
Sleep disturbances
Lethargy
Gastrointestinal distress
Respiratory problems
Phobias, panic reactions
Nightmares
Eating disorders
Dermatological reactions

CHANGES IN SELF-PERCEPTION
Poor self-concept or self-esteem
Lack of competency
Powerlessness
Isolation

SOCIAL, INTERPERSONAL RELATEDNESS, AND SEXUAL EFFECTS
Withdrawal
Fear of new people
Lack of trust
Change in physical appearance
Change in social network patterns
Negative attitudes about sexual relationships

Adapted from M. A. Paludi and R. B. Barickman, *Academic and Workplace Sexual Harassment: A Resource Manual* (Albany: State University of New York Press, 1991). By permission of the State University of New York Press. © 1991.

Avoidance
>Individual attempts to avoid situation by staying away from the harasser

Assertion or confrontation
>Individual refuses sexual or social offers or verbally confronts the harasser

Seeking institutional or organizational relief
>Individual reports the incident and files a complaint

Social support
>Individual seeks support of others to validate perceptions of the behaviors

Appeasement
>Individual attempts to evade the harasser without confrontation; attempts to placate the harasser

Ormerod and Gold, using this classification system, noted that internal strategies represented by far the most common response overall.[25] Most victims do not tell the harasser to stop. Their initial attempts to manage the initiator are rarely direct. Typically harassers are more powerful physically and organizationally than the victims, and sometimes the harasser's intentions are unclear. The first or first several harassing events are often ignored by victims—especially when they are experiencing hostile environment sexual harassment where the behavior may be more subtle. Victims may interpret or reinterpret the situation so that the incident is not defined as sexual harassment. Many times victims ignore the perpetrator.

Victims (especially women of color) of sexual harassment may fear retaliation should they confront the harasser. The economic reality for most women is that they can't just leave a workplace where they are being sexually harassed. Women and men do not want their livelihoods threatened. They are serious about work. They do not enjoy experiencing sexual harassment.

Sexual Harassment: Issues across the Life Cycle

Thus far in our discussion, we have summarized research and theories dealing with sexual harassment of women and men in the workplace. As most human-resource managers and therapists know, sexual harassment that happens to employees is very similar to what occurred to these same individuals as students. Consequently, a great deal of research has been exploring the incidence and psychological dimensions of sexual harassment in schools, colleges, and universities. We now present an overview of the issues we discussed in this chapter specifically with respect to students. It is important to consider individuals' prior experiences with sexual harassment. They can help us understand whether individuals use an internally or externally focused strategy in dealing with sexual harassment in the workplace.

INCIDENCE OF SEXUAL HARASSMENT OF STUDENTS

Research has suggested that, similar to employees, most students do not label their experiences as sexual harassment despite the fact the behavior they have experienced meets the legal definition of either *quid pro quo* or hostile-environment harassment.[26] The American Association of University Women studied 1,632 students in grades eight through eleven from seventy-nine schools across the United States.[27] Students were asked, "During your whole school life, how often, if at all, has anyone (this includes students, teachers, other school employees, or anyone else) done the following things to you *when you did not want them to?*"

Made sexual comments, jokes, gestures, or looks.

Showed, gave, or left you sexual pictures, photographs, illustrations, messages, or notes.

Wrote sexual messages or graffiti about you on bathroom walls, in locker rooms, etc.

Spread sexual rumors about you.

Said you were gay or lesbian.

Spied on you as you dressed or showered at school.

Flashed or "mooned" you.

Touched, grabbed, or pinched you in a sexual way.

Pulled at your clothing in a sexual way.

Intentionally brushed against you in a sexual way.

Pulled your clothing off or down.

Blocked your way or cornered you in a sexual way.

Forced you to kiss him or her.

Forced you to do something sexual, other than kissing.

Results suggested that four out of five students (81 percent) reported that they have been the target of some form of sexual harassment during their school lives. With respect to gender comparisons, 85 percent of girls and 76 percent of boys surveyed reported they have experienced unwelcomed sexual behavior that interferes with their ability to concentrate at school and with their personal lives. The AAUW study also analyzed for race comparisons. African American boys (81 percent) were more likely to have experienced sexual harassment than white boys (75 percent) and Latinos (69 percent). For girls, 87 percent of whites reported having experienced behaviors that constitute sexual harassment, compared with 84 percent of African American girls and 82 percent of Latinas.

The AAUW study also suggested that adolescents' experiences with sexual harassment are most likely to occur in the middle school or junior high school years of sixth to ninth grade. The behaviors reported by students, in order from most experienced to least experienced, include the following:

Sexual comments, jokes, gestures, or looks

Touched, grabbed, or pinched in a sexual way

Intentionally brushed against in a sexual way

Flashed or "mooned"

Had sexual rumors spread about them

Had clothing pulled at in a sexual way

Shown, given, or left sexual pictures, photographs, illustrations, messages, or notes

Had their way blocked or were cornered in a sexual way

Had sexual messages or graffiti written about them on bathroom walls, in locker rooms, etc.

Forced to kiss someone

Called gay or lesbian

Had clothing pulled off or down

Forced to do something sexual, other than kissing

Spied on as they dressed or showered at school.

Students reported that they experience these behaviors while in the classroom or in the hallways as they are going to class. Although the majority of harassment in schools is student-to-student, 25 percent of harassed girls and 10 percent of boys reported they were harassed by teachers or other school employees.

With respect to the incidence of sexual harassment of college and university students, Dziech and Weiner reported that 30 percent of undergraduate women suffer sexual harassment from at least one of their instructors during the women's four years of college.[28] When definitions of sexual harassment include sexist remarks and other forms of gender harassment, the incidence in undergraduate populations nears 70 percent.[29]

Bailey and Richards reported that of 246 women graduate students in their sample, 13 percent indicated they had been sexually harassed, 21 percent had not enrolled in a course to avoid such behavior, and 16 percent indicated they had been directly assaulted.[30] Bond (1988) reported that 75 percent of the 229 women who responded to her survey experienced jokes with sexual themes during their graduate training, 69 percent were subjected to sexist comments demeaning to women, and 58 percent reported experiencing sexist remarks about their clothing, body, or sexual activities.[31]

Fitzgerald, Shullman, Bailey, Richards, Swecker, Gold, Ormerod, and Weitzman investigated approximately two thousand women at two major state universities.[32] Half of the women respondents reported experiencing some form of sexually harassing behavior. The majority of these women reported experiencing sexist comments by faculty. The next largest category of sexually harassing behavior was seductive behavior, including being invited for drinks and a backrub by faculty members, being brushed up against by their professors, and having their professors show up uninvited at their hotel rooms during out-of-town academic conferences or conventions.

Research by Paludi, DeFour, and Roberts[33] suggests that the incidence of academic sexual harassment of ethnic minority women students is even greater than that reported by white women. Dziech and Weiner[34] and De-Four[35] suggested that ethnic minority women are more vulnerable to receiving sexual attention from professors. Ethnic minority women are subject to stereotypes about sex, are viewed as mysterious, and are less sure of themselves in their careers. Thus, although all students are vulnerable to some degree, male teachers and faculty tend to select those who are most vulnerable and needy. For certain student groups, the incidence of sexual harassment appears to be higher than others.[36] For example:

Girls and women of color, especially those with "token" status

Graduate students, whose future careers are often determined by their association with a particular faculty member

Students in small colleges or small academic departments, where the number of faculty available to students is quite small

Girl and women students in male-populated fields (e.g., engineering)

Students who are economically disadvantaged and work part time or full time while attending classes

Lesbian women, who may be harassed as part of homophobia

Physically or emotionally disabled students

Women students who work in dormitories as resident assistants

Girls and women who have been sexually abused

Inexperienced, unassertive, socially isolated girls and women, who may appear more vulnerable and appealing to those who would intimidate or entice them into an exploitive relationship.

Schools most likely to have a high incidence of sexual harassment are ones, according to research,[37] that

Have no policy prohibiting sexual harassment

Do not disseminate the policy or report information regarding sexual harassment

Have no training programs for teachers, staff, and students

Do not intervene officially when sexual harassment occurs

Do not support sexual harassment victims

Do not quickly remove sexual graffiti

Do not sanction individuals who engage in sexual harassment

Do not inform the school community about the sanctions for offenders

Have been previously all-male or have a majority of male students.

Sexual harassment is thus a major form of victimization of students in our system of higher education.

From the Psychology Laboratory to the Workplace: Using Psychological Research and Theories to Deal With Sexual Harassment

The psychological research and theories we have summarized thus far have tremendous implications for dealing with sexual harassment in the workplace.

For example, the research on women's and men's differential perceptions of identical behavior suggests the need for training programs to include units on attributions and attitudes about women's and men's verbal and nonverbal communication styles. Because women tend to view sexual harassment as an abuse of power and men tend to view sexual harassment as flirtation and flattery, both sexes should be present in training sessions together. In training sessions, many women are pleased that the issue will finally be addressed; many men are worried that they can't joke or have fun with women anymore. It is helpful to include women and men in the same training sessions so that these differential perceptions can be identified and discussed.

Separate sessions for women and men may perpetuate stereotypes that all men are guilty of sexual harassment and all women are victims. This latter type of training is also divisive and contributes to further harassment of women by men. Both women and men have the same rights and responsibilities with respect to sexual harassment and must be provided the same information concerning these rights and responsibilities.

In addition to integrating psychological research and theories into training programs for employees, this information must be taken into account in the policy statements and grievance procedures. In part II of this book we discuss effective policy statements and grievance procedures on sexual harassment, viewing the issue from both the perspectives of the recipient and initiator.

Summary

In this chapter we reviewed the current research and theories from the field of psychology on workplace sexual harassment. In our discussion, we reviewed the literature on women's and men's perceptions of identical behavior, their attributions and attitudes about sexual harassment, and how they cope with this form of victimization—either internally or externally. We also addressed the need to view sexual harassment along a life-cycle perspective and addressed the incidence and dimensions of sexual harassment during junior high school, high school, and college.

From our review of sexual harassment from the psychology perspective, we can summarize the following:

> Sexual harassment can be viewed as an abuse of power and the reflection of the low status of individuals in the workplace.

> Many individuals cling to the myth that sexual harassment includes only physical assault. In fact, sexual harassment is far more pervasive than sexual assault.

> Sexual harassment is unwelcome sexual advances or requests for sexual favors. Sexual harassment also includes other verbal or physical conduct of a sexual nature.

> Although generalizations are difficult given the nature of the available data, it does appear reasonable to estimate that one out of every two women will be harassed at some point in her work history.

> Research suggests that as women approach numerical parity in various segments of the workforce, sexual harassment may decline.

> Men may experience sexual harassment as well, but the incidence for women is greater than that for men.

> Most victims do not use an externally focused strategy for dealing with sexual harassment.

> Victims of sexual harassment fear retaliation should they confront the harasser.

> Women may not label their experiences as sexual harassment, despite the fact that the experiences meet the legal definition of this form of victimization. Consequently, they may not label their stress-related responses as being caused or exacerbated by the sexual harassment.

> Sexual harassment has a radiating impact and can thus affect the working experiences of all women and men in an organization.

For Reflection

1. Discuss the difference between legal and empirically derived definitions of sexual harassment.
2. Define the following empirically derived categories of sexual harassment:
   Gender harassment
   Seductive behavior
   Sexual bribery
   Sexual coercion
   Sexual imposition
3. Discuss what is meant in the psychological literature by the term *formal power differential.*

4. Provide examples of verbal forms of sexual harassment.

5. Provide examples of physical forms of sexual harassment.

6. Discuss the results of the 1981 study conducted by the United States Merit Systems Protection Board.

7. Identify occupational group differences in sexual harassment.

8. What is a gender stereotype? Give an example of a gender stereotype related to a woman and to a man.

9. Cite examples of the operation of gender stereotypes in the workplace.

10. Discuss the relationship between masculine aggression and sexual harassment.

11. What explanatory model offered do you believe best explains sexual harassment in the workplace? Cite evidence for your position.

12. Outline some of the symptoms common to the Sexual Harassment Trauma Syndrome.

13. Discuss the difference between internally and externally focused strategies for dealing with sexual harassment.

14. Discuss the results of the 1993 American Association of University Women study with adolescents.

15. Discuss the incidence and psychological dimensions of sexual harassment among college and university students.

Notes

1. Adapted from M. A. PALUDI & R. B. BARICKMAN, ACADEMIC AND WORKPLACE SEXUAL HARASSMENT: A MANUAL OF RESOURCES (1991). By permission of the State University of New York Press. © 1991.

2. F. TILL, SEXUAL HARASSMENT: A REPORT ON THE SEXUAL HARASSMENT OF STUDENTS (1980).

3. L. F. Fitzgerald & A. Ormerod, *Sexual Harassment in Academia and the Workplace, in* PSYCHOLOGY OF WOMEN: A HANDBOOK OF ISSUES AND THEORIES 556 (F. Denmark & M. Paludi eds., 1993).

4. IVORY POWER: SEXUAL HARASSMENT ON CAMPUS (M. A. Paludi ed., 1990).

5. U.S. MERIT SYSTEMS PROTECTION BOARD, SEXUAL HARASSMENT OF FEDERAL WORKERS: IS IT A PROBLEM? (1981).U.S. MERIT SYSTEMS PROTECTION BOARD, SEXUAL HARASSMENT OF FEDERAL WORKERS: AN UPDATE (1987).

6. B. GUTEK, SEX AND THE WORKPLACE (1985).

7. L. F. Fitzgerald et al., *The Incidence and Dimensions of Sexual Harassment in Academia and the Workplace,* JOURNAL OF VOCATIONAL BEHAVIOR 32, at 152–175.

8. Y. Gold, The Sexualization of the Workplace: Sexual Harassment of Pink-, White-, and Blue-Collar Workers, paper presented to the annual conference of the American Psychological Association (August 1987).

9. E. LaFontaine & L. Tredeau, *The Frequency, Sources, and Correlates of Sexual Harassment among Women in Traditional Male Occupations,* SEX ROLES 15, at 423–432.

10. N. Baker, Sexual Harassment and Job Satisfaction in Traditional and Nontraditional Industrial Occupations (1989) (unpublished Ph.D. dissertation, California School of Professional Psychology Los Angeles).

11. B. GUTEK, SEX AND THE WORKPLACE (1985).

12. J. DOYLE & M. PALUDI, SEX AND GENDER: THE HUMAN EXPERIENCE (3d ed. 1995).

13. M. A. PALUDI, THE PSYCHOLOGY OF WOMEN (1992).

14. B. Lott, *The Perils and Promise of Studying Sexist Discrimination in Face-to-Face Situations, in* IVORY POWER: SEXUAL HARASSMENT ON CAMPUS (M. Paludi ed., 1990).

15. Reprinted from K. Quina, *The Victimization of Women, in* IVORY POWER: SEXUAL HARASSMENT ON CAMPUS (M. Paludi ed., 1990). By permission of the State University of New York Press. © 1990.

16. M. A. Paludi, research in progress (1995).

17. L. F. Fitzgerald & L. Weitzman, *Men Who Harass: Speculation and Data, in* IVORY POWER: SEXUAL HARASSMENT ON CAMPUS (M. Paludi ed., 1990).

18. J. Pryor, *Sexual Harassment Proclivities in Men,* SEX ROLES 17, at 269–290.

19. S. Tangri et al., *Sexual Harassment at Work: Three Explanatory Models,* JOURNAL OF SOCIAL ISSUES 38, at 33–54.

20. L. F. Fitzgerald & A. Ormerod, *Sexual Harassment in Academia and the Workplace, in* PSYCHOLOGY OF WOMEN: A HANDBOOK OF ISSUES AND THEORIES (F. Denmark & M. Paludi eds., 1993).

21. K. Quina, *The Victimization of Women, in* IVORY POWER: SEXUAL HARASSMENT ON CAMPUS (M. Paludi ed., 1990. V. C. Rabinowitz, *Coping with Sexual Harassment, in* IVORY POWER: SEXUAL HARASSMENT ON CAMPUS (M. Paludi ed., 1990).

22. P. Crull, *Stress Effects of Sexual Harassment on the Job: Implications for Counseling,* AMERICAN JOURNAL OF ORTHOPSYCHIATRY 52, at 539–544. V. C. Rabinowitz, *Coping with Sexual Harassment, in* IVORY POWER: SEXUAL HARASSMENT ON CAMPUS (M. Paludi ed., 1990).

23. New York Division of Human Rights, *Survey of the Costs of Sexual Harassment, in* SEXUAL HARASSMENT: BUILDING A CONSENSUS FOR CHANGE (J. Avner, Chairperson, 1993).

24. L. F. Fitzgerald et al., *Responses to Victimization: Validation of an Objective Policy,* JOURNAL OF COLLEGE STUDENT PERSONNEL 27, at 34–39.

25. A. Ormerod & Y. Gold, Coping with Sexual Harassment: Internal and External Strategies for Coping with Stress, paper presented to the annual conference of the Association for Women in Psychology (March 1988).

26. IVORY POWER: SEXUAL HARASSMENT ON CAMPUS (M. A. Paludi ed., 1990).

27. AMERICAN ASSOCIATION OF UNIVERSITY WOMEN, HOSTILE HALLWAYS (1993).

28. B. DZIECH & L. WEINER, THE LECHEROUS PROFESSOR (1984).

29. IVORY POWER: SEXUAL HARASSMENT ON CAMPUS (M. A. Paludi ed., 1990).

30. N. Bailey & M. Richards, Tarnishing the Ivory Tower: Sexual Harassment in Graduate Training Programs in Psychology, paper presented at the annual meeting of the American Psychological Association (August 1985).

31. M. Bond, *Division 27 Sexual Harassment Survey: Definition, Impact, and Environmental Context,* COMMUNITY PSYCHOLOGIST 21, at 7–10.

32. L. F. Fitzgerald et al., *The Incidence and Dimensions of Sexual Harassment in Academia and the Workplace,* JOURNAL OF VOCATIONAL BEHAVIOR 32, at 152–175.

33. M. A. Paludi, D. C. DeFour, & R. Roberts, Academic Sexual Harassment of Ethnic Minority Women (1994) (research in progress).

34. B. DZIECH & L. WEINER. THE LECHEROUS PROFESSOR (1984).

35. D. C. DeFour, *The Interface of Racism and Sexism on College Campuses, in* IVORY POWER: SEXUAL HARASSMENT ON CAMPUS (M. Paludi ed., 1990).

36. R. B. Barickman et al., *Sexual Harassment of Students: Victims of the College Experience, in* VICTIMOLOGY: AN INTERNATIONAL PERSPECTIVE (E. Viano ed., 1992).

37. B. SANDLER & M. PALUDI, EDUCATOR'S GUIDE TO CONTROLLING SEXUAL HARASSMENT (1993).

PART

2

Preventing Sexual Harassment in the Workplace

Avoiding Liability through an Effective Policy

I, and I suppose every member of this committee, have to come down to the ultimate question of who is telling the truth. My experience as a lawyer and a judge is that you listen to all the testimony and then you try to determine the motivation for the one that is not telling the truth.

—Senator Heflin,
Senate Judiciary Confirmation Hearings
of Clarence Thomas, 1991

CASE STUDY

The following policy was just issued at a large manufacturing company:

It is the policy of Consolidated Dermatics that all employees be able to enjoy a work environment free from all forms of discrimination, including sexual harassment. No employee, either male or female, should be subjected to discrimination.

Sexual harassment does not refer to occasional compliments of a socially acceptable nature. It refers to: (1) unwelcome sexual

---

advances or requests for sexual favors or other verbal or physical conduct when submission to such conduct is made either explicitly or implicitly a term or condition of an individual's employment, (2) submission to or rejection of such conduct by an individual is used as the basis for employment decisions affecting such individual, or (3) such conduct has the purpose or effect of unreasonably interfering with an individual's work performance or creating an intimidating or hostile work environment.

Each supervisor has a responsibility to maintain the workplace free from discrimination. This includes discussing this policy with employees and assuring them that they are not to endure insulting, degrading, or exploitive sexual treatment. Given the nature of sexual harassment, the company will also treat very seriously any allegations or accusations that are found to be false.

PROCEDURE

Any employee who believes he or she has been the subject of discrimination, including sexual harassment, should report the alleged incident immediately to his or her supervisor and also to the director of personnel. An investigation will be undertaken immediately, and any employee who has been found by the company to have discriminated against another employee will be subject to appropriate sanctions.

Any questions about this policy or the procedure should be directed to your supervisor or to Marvin Donner, director of personnel.

Legally speaking, is this a good policy? Are there areas where it could be improved? How would the courts view this policy if a lawsuit is brought against the company for sexual harassment?

Introduction

As has been seen in earlier chapters, sexual harassment is a particularly troublesome type of job discrimination. Some people contend that it involves the "normal" social interaction between the sexes and are resistant to changing behavior that has been ingrained through the years. Because such reticence is not a defense to a charge of sexual harassment, a company must find ways to deal with it in an effective, efficient manner. Usually this means putting together a policy and procedure that works—not an easy task because of the unique nature of the phenomenon. It is not an impossible task, though, and companies that are serious about the problem are reporting great success in rooting it out through effective, comprehensive programs. The matter must be approached seriously and with a firm resolve, or any undertaking will be doomed to failure. Success requires action to prevent *and* remedy sexual harassment, as well as to train the entire workforce on the various aspects of the issue.

Policies and *Quid Pro Quo* Harassment

As was discussed in chapter 2, when a person with authority abuses that authority by making unwelcomed threats or promises of benefits in exchange for sexual favors, the employer is in a very difficult situation. There is little, if anything, that can be done to avoid liability. The courts and the EEOC consider these situations as strict liability situations; in other words, despite any policy and procedures the company may have against this type of behavior, if it happens, the employer is liable. A business should try to prevent this type of harassment with appropriate training and sanctions, but if an investigation shows that such harassment occurred, the company should do whatever it can to remedy the problem for the affected employee. At that point, the company should also strongly consider removing the offending manager from the workplace before more trouble occurs.

Policies and Hostile Environment Harassment

Hostile environment situations operate somewhat differently with regard to employer liability. Because businesses are not strictly liable in those situations, businesses have the opportunity to take affirmative actions that will limit the potential for lawsuits and legal liability. The courts and the EEOC have put great emphasis on the need for effective, workable, and fail-safe policies and procedures for the elimination of sexual harassment, and cases in which employers have these in place are now being dismissed.

AN OVERVIEW OF AN EFFECTIVE POLICY

A good policy requires more than a statement of compliance with the law. A policy must be designed to both prevent harassment and remedy any that might occur. Many courts have noted that cases might never have come before them if the employer had taken care of the problem by instituting a sexual harassment policy and carrying it out in an appropriate manner. In *Meritor Savings Bank v. Vinson,* the Supreme Court made it clear that effective policies and procedures need to be carefully thought out. As the Justices stated, the Court did not accept the argument that "the mere existence of a grievance procedure and a policy against discrimination, coupled with the respondent's failure to invoke that procedure"[1] protected an employer from liability.

What then must a policy and procedure include? As a starting point, it is helpful to look at the EEOC's guidelines, which lay down the framework for the goals of an effective program:

> Prevention is the best tool for the elimination of sexual harassment. An employer should take all steps necessary to prevent sexual harassment from occurring, such as affirmatively raising the subject, expressing strong disapproval, developing appropriate sanctions, informing employees of their right to raise and how to raise the issue of harassment under title VII, and developing methods to sensitize all concerned.

Obviously, however, this is just a framework. Cases in which courts have made comments about the adequacy or, more usually, the inadequacy of a policy help to fill out this structure. In at least one case, *Robinson v. Jacksonville Shipyards,*[2] the court supervised the design of a policy and procedure, giving employers an excellent example to follow.

Although many businesses may believe that their current policies are adequate, investigations are revealing that many are sadly deficient in important areas. Although no particular form is necessary, there are certain aspects that courts continually look for and that will help a business eliminate problems long before a court or government agency even has to look at the policy. A paragraph expressing disapproval is clearly inadequate in today's legal climate; the policy approved by the court in *Robinson* required the company to put together a veritable manual, many pages in length.

KEY ELEMENTS IN AN EFFECTIVE POLICY

There are several important elements of an effective policy and procedure. A company that pays attention to each of these will be doing what is necessary in order to put together a program that will both meet the needs of employees and managers and stand the ultimate test in court, if that should ever become necessary. Note though that if the policy is designed to do what it would be tested for—its ability to prevent and handle problems before they get out of control—a court test will probably never result.

Setting an Appropriate Tone   An overriding consideration for any sexual harassment policy is whether it sets a tone of appropriate seriousness and concern for the employees' rights. There are many ways that this is accomplished, including making sure that *everyone* from the lowest-level workers to the highest-level managers knows of the seriousness of the matter and of his or her responsibility in carrying out this policy.

Creating a Separate Sexual Harassment Policy   The courts have made it clear that a general policy against discrimination is inadequate with regard to sexual harassment liability. Because sexual harassment presents unique problems with regard to identifying problem behavior and reporting requirements, the EEOC has supported the view that a separate policy needs to be adopted. Thus, a sexual harassment policy must be clearly identified with procedures that may differ, if necessary, from the normal complaint procedures in effect at the company.

> *In the case study, the company has a general-purpose policy, rather than a specific policy designed for eradicating sexual harassment. A court may deem this policy inadequate if it is challenged in a complaint or lawsuit.*

Expressing Strong Disapproval   It is not enough to state that sexual harassment is forbidden. The policy must communicate the company's serious and strong disapproval of any such behavior or conduct. The seriousness of the company's commitment should be made clear in the choice of language used and in the comprehensiveness of the program. Giving a high-level person with strong authority ultimate responsibility for carrying out this policy and communicating that fact to the employees is also a good way to show the seriousness with which the company views this matter. Employees are very perceptive. They will take seriously only those matters that the management takes seriously, and they can see through perfunctory attempts at compliance with the law. If the workforce believes that this is a very important matter to the company and that it will be dealt with in an appropriate manner, many potential harassers will fall into line.

> *In the case study, the person identified with the policy appears to be Marvin Donner, the director of personnel. It is important that Donner be someone of authority who is known to be respected by the employees and the company higher-ups. Workers know that "big jobs" go to "big people" and will draw inferences about the employer's commitment from the people named in the policy. Perhaps the CEO should be listed or should write a letter to accompany the policy.*

Encouraging Reports   It is not enough that the policy *allows* for a reporting of behavior or conduct. According to the United States Supreme Court and the EEOC, the policy must *encourage* victims to come forward. This can be specifically stated, but the tone of the policy will really make the difference between allowing and encouraging conduct reports.

It is a good idea to preface the policy with a statement that the company is not just dealing with sexual harassment because it presents the potential for legal problems. By stating that harassment has no place in the company, serves no business purpose, and that the well-being of the employees is important to management, the employer is telling the employees that they work in a place where people care about more than their productivity. This creates an atmosphere where employees see their problems as important to their managers, and an environment where everyone will feel comfortable resisting or reporting inappropriate and unwelcome behavior.

Because of this need to encourage victims to come forward, it is not a good idea to specifically include in any sexual harassment policy a statement about false claims. Although no organization will want to encourage false claims, such a statement has been shown to have what the law calls a "chilling" effect. This means that such a statement's discouraging effect on the reporting of *true* claims far outweighs its value in eliminating *untrue* claims. It is often very difficult for an employee to come forward, and studies show that women in particular often do not expect to be believed when they report harassing behavior. Statements about retribution for false claims may reinforce feelings by some harassed employees that the harasser will accuse them of lying, the higher-ups will believe the perpetrator, and severe consequences will follow. Thus, statements about false claims are not advisable. They could make a policy less than encouraging and, in fact, inhospitable to victims.

According to most investigators, false claims are not a great problem, although, of course, they do occur and should be dealt with appropriately when they are discovered. Any benefits to be gained from including language about what are probably isolated situations are far outweighed by the negative effects of such language.

> *The case study has language about false claims. The company should consider whether it makes the policy sound forbidding and more carefully think about including it.*

Clarifying Prohibited Conduct   Employees and managers must know what they are expected to do or not do. As chapters 2 and 3 make clear, it is not easy to define the exact parameters of sexual harassment, and the law continues to expand the definition. It is possible to give an understanding, however, by a general description of the various types and some examples.

Specifics   The big question with regard to testing if a policy communicates clearly is whether all of the people in the workplace understand exactly what type of behavior or conduct is being prohibited. A company must tell its employees in no uncertain terms. There is no good business purpose in being evasive, and evasive language can only result in an inadequate policy. If an employer makes it clear that the examples given are just examples and that prohibited conduct can take many forms, there will be no problem with workers thinking that they have a comprehensive list of what can't be done and that everything else is fair game.

Retaliation   A policy should specifically point out that retaliation is a form of sexual harassment and a violation of the policy. Some companies like to restrict this prohibition to retaliation for *true* reports of sexual harassment. Once again, this is not advisable, even though an employee might try to claim that discipline for a false report is retaliation in violation of the company policy. Carefully worded, however, a nonretaliation provision will allow for discipline for false reports because the report was not, in fact, a report of sexual harassment.

If discipline for false reports is to be a part of the program, investigators should be careful to distinguish between a report without adequate evidence (or the mistaken belief that inappropriate behavior was going on) and the intentional filing of a false report.

The case study policy does not mention retaliation as prohibited conduct, and workers could claim that they were unaware that retaliation was not allowed. Making it clear will solve that problem.

Using Understandable Language and Terms   It is a good idea to begin with the EEOC's definition of sexual harassment. A mistake made by many companies, however, is to think that this, by itself, is adequate. No one, including lawyers, can gain a good understanding of sexual harassment merely from reading the very legalistic and convoluted language contained in the guidelines. Thus, employees should not be expected to do so either. Certainly, it is clear that sexual harassment has a legal definition, and lawyers will continue to use it as the basis for lawsuits; a company's policy, however, is not being written for lawyers or judges. It is being written for people of varying intellectual abilities and educational backgrounds, and all of them need to understand it.

The case study policy does contain the EEOC definition but nothing further. How likely are the members of the workforce to understand this legalese? Does the coldness of the definition take away from an encouraging tone?

The policy ordered by the court in *Robinson* used the following language: "The management of Jacksonville Shipyards, Inc., considers the following conduct to represent some of the types of acts which violate JSI's Sexual Harassment Policy." The policy then goes on to list a series of examples under headings ranging from physical assaults of a sexual nature to sexual or discriminatory displays or publications anywhere in the workplace to retaliation for sexual harassment complaints. As stated previously, it is vital that the policy gives specific examples of each type of harassment and that the policy specifically singles out retaliation as a form of harassment and identifies it as prohibited conduct. Retaliation, in the *Robinson* policy's definition of the term, can take many forms, including pressuring someone to drop a complaint, refusing to cooperate with an investigation, or falsely denying a complaint. It may, in fact, be better described to employees as retaliation or obstruction of an investigation.

What is missing from the *Robinson* policy is a listing of conduct that, although not sexual in nature, is still a form of gender harassment. Such conduct would include demeaning comments, general statements about the inadequacy of people of certain genders to perform certain tasks, and joking about the difficulty a person of one gender may have performing certain duties (e.g., a woman who must exert more effort to lift a required weight).

Explaining the Concept of *Unwelcome*   A business should help its employees to differentiate between a socially acceptable, polite compliment or overture for a date and sexual harassment by reinforcing that the basis for finding that conduct is harassment is that the conduct is unwelcome. It should be carefully noted, however, that this is not always easy to determine, and that silence or the fact that someone appears to be joining in should not necessarily be taken to mean that conduct is welcome. The policy should include a statement that clearly states that employees should presume that any sexual or demeaning comments, behavior, displays, and publications are unwelcome, and also that, once a polite compliment or overture for a date has been turned down or any manifestation given that such behavior is not wanted, the overtures should immediately cease.

The policy in the case study uses the term unwelcome, *but does not explain it. This may not be helpful to the workers, who may not understand what* unwelcome *means or how it may be manifested.*

Prohibiting Harassment Regardless of the Source   Under today's view of hostile environment harassment, it is fairly certain that an employer will be liable no matter who is perpetrating the harassing conduct. A company's policy should clearly state that employees need not endure unwelcome overtures, comments, glances, or any other behavior, whether it is from a co-worker, supervisor, manager from another department, customer, client, supplier, or salesperson. Employees should be assured that any violation of the policy, no matter who is involved, will be dealt with in a serious manner and appropriate action will be taken. A policy should state specifically that no one, no matter how highly placed in the organization, is exempt from these requirements or from being disciplined accordingly for violations.

Describing the Process for Reporting Violations   Because the policy and procedures should be designed to both prevent and remedy harassment, a company must put a system into place that will make employees feel comfortable in reporting problems. As previously stated, the courts and the EEOC continue to demand that the procedures be designed to encourage victims to come forward, not merely to allow them to report.

Creating Fail-Safe Procedures   The best advice with regard to deciding who should receive reports about sexual harassment is to give ultimate responsibility to someone who has authority and the respect of other workers. A business should make this a fail-safe system, however, by giving the employees alternates for reporting. These alternatives may include the employee's own supervisor, but for several reasons, courts and the EEOC have stated that procedures that *require* complaining first to the next in command will be deemed ineffective. The supervisor may be the offending party or may not be someone with whom the employee feels comfortable. In fact, if many employees tend to opt to report elsewhere, a prudent employer will use this as evidence that this manager may not be handling sexual harassment in an appropriate manner and should take steps to handle this problem. Although a requirement that employees go through channels is appropriate in the workplace in most respects, it is not advisable in sexual harassment situations. An employer can best get a handle on any problems by making it as easy as possible for complainants to come forward.

Because it has been proven that talking about sexual harassment is difficult, especially for women, some thought should be given to naming at least one woman who has the authority to receive complaints. As with all parties involved in the process, the responsible people must be given adequate authority to go forward with complaints and training to sensitively receive them.

The case study policy does provide that behavior be reported to the supervisor and the director of personnel. If this was an alternate reporting procedure, it would be much better. As written, this chain-of-command requirement is a major flaw in the policy. The policy has also not identified a woman who is authorized to receive complaints. This may be seen as allowing, rather than encouraging, reports.

Specifying Complete Complaint Procedures   A policy should not just give the title of the people, beyond the employee's own supervisor, who are designated to handle complaints. Although top managers may be well aware of the identity of the director of human relations, in large companies, especially, employees in the lower echelons may know only that he or she exists in some large office at the other end of the building. The company should specifically list the person who is in charge of the policy and to whom complaints may be addressed, giving the name, phone number, and office location. In addition, a statement should be included assuring anyone who wishes to speak to this person that they should feel comfortable requesting an interview and that they will be accommodated, as much as possible, with regard to work or other scheduling considerations.

How would someone find Donner, in the case study company? Does everyone know who he is or where to find him? Probably not.

Reports by Anyone   It must be made clear that providing a universally conducive workplace is everyone's responsibility and that everyone has a right to feel comfortable in the work environment. Thus a worker need not be the direct focus of harassing behavior to come forward and report the problem. Third parties should be urged to file a report, even if they are unsure about the potential victim's feelings about the behavior. A policy should state that an investigation will be undertaken to determine whether there is a problem, and that a determination of whether the conduct was welcomed need not be made before reporting. It must be remembered, however, that conduct that is determined to be welcomed by the employee who is the focus of the harassment may still be contributing to a hostile environment for the third party and may have to be dealt with in any case.

Oral or Written Reports   Although it is preferable to have a written report by the person lodging the complaint, some workers do not feel comfortable expressing themselves in writing. It is also possible that some workers may not be able to read or write, or have some learning disability that does not allow them to file written reports. (This is why it is advisable to orally go over the policy with all workers and explain it to them.) Thus, to encourage reporting, oral reports should be allowed. The person to whom the report is orally given may take notes about the situation during the interview. The notes can be reviewed for accuracy with the person making the complaint.

Anonymous Complaints   There are certainly some problems involved in allowing reports of harassing behavior without requiring the identity of the person making the complaint. As businesses find when they use suggestion boxes, however, it is often possible to learn a great deal more about the real situation when a specific individual need not be associated with the report. This is to the employer's benefit with regard to sexual harassment, when remedying problems and preventing escalation is paramount in avoiding extensive liability and high legal costs. Anonymous complaints encourage reporting.

Anonymous reports can be carefully handled to minimize the possibility of them being used for vindictive or other purposes. If anonymous reports are allowed, a company may wish to state that the anonymous reports may be handled in a different manner from identified reports. Whereas investigations may be undertaken if reports are deemed to be credible, the investigations may be on a more informal basis. In addition, remedies could be different, as dismissal without an identified report, for example, would be unlikely.

A company should encourage people to give their names and, if too many anonymous complaints come in, try to determine why. Is there something about the workplace or the procedures that make people afraid to give their names? Such a situation must be remedied. Anonymous complaint procedures will be discussed again in chapter 5.

Describing the Investigation Process   The potential participant will always feel more encouraged to become involved in a process when he or she understands what the process entails. Fear of the unknown can discourage reporting. Every workplace will have its own way of handling complaints based on its structure, the size of its staff, and other considerations, but an explanation of the process, whatever it is, is important. Certain elements should be involved in every process.

Employees should be assured that reports will be taken seriously and that an investigation will be undertaken promptly by someone trained to handle such situations. Then the promise must be carried out. It is not good to delay or put off an investigation for any reason other than the request of the complaining party. The courts and the EEOC mean it when they say that immediate action is required. This requires that, within a few days of receiving a report, the process should begin, and a final report and remedial action should be undertaken within a week or two at the most. Unremedied situations have a way of getting out of hand, and this is something that should be avoided at all costs.

Ensuring confidentiality—as much as is possible—is also important. Employees must believe, with good basis, that once a report is made, it will not become the subject of workplace gossip. The procedures should be designed to maintain secrecy, and the employees should be made aware of that. This requires that those involved in the investigation be made very aware of the need to keep all information as confidential as possible. Anyone who is informed of the complaint or any part of the investigation must be told only on a needs-to-know basis. Separate locked files should be kept for records on complaints and investigations, with the keys carefully controlled. Everyone who is at all involved, from the investigator to the secretary who types the reports to the clerk who files them, should be trained to keep the information secret and told that any violations will be deemed and handled as very serious matters.

Employees must be told that it will be impossible to keep the report totally secret because there will have to be interviews with the alleged harasser and with any witnesses identified by either party. The policy should note, however, that in every way possible the confidentiality of the report will be paramount in the process. Investigators should look carefully at all parts of the process to ensure that this promise is kept. Are there soundproof, separate rooms for investigations? How will the company ensure that gossip doesn't center around people who enter that room? Who will be involved in the investigation, and have they been adequately trained with regard to confidentiality? These and other questions must be carefully examined because the courts and the EEOC will be looking not just at what a company says it will do, but also whether, in fact, it does it.

Complainants must believe that they will be treated with respect and in a serious manner. A trained investigator would not joke or make lighthearted comments during an interview. The investigator should not address a complainant by his or her first name, unless invited to do so, wander in and out of the interview room, or smile inappropriately. Employees should be told that they should expect a serious investigation and that this is what will happen. They will be treated with respect and should expect nothing less.

> *The case study policy does not adequately describe the process for investigation. The employees at the company do not know what to expect if they file a complaint and may not be* encouraged *to do so.*

Ensuring Follow-Up Procedures   Once the investigation is completed and remedial measures taken, if appropriate, the complainants should not feel that they are on their own. They must be reassured by a description of the follow-up procedures. These procedures should involve, at a minimum, inquiries to make sure that harassment has not resumed and that the complainant has not suffered any retaliation. As always, it is vital not just to say that a follow-up will occur, but rather to actually carry this out in every case.

Describing Penalties and Discipline   It is important to assure workers that the process is designed to *make them whole,* a legal term that means that they should not suffer any lasting consequences from the harassment. They must not be transferred without their consent; they must not be required to take an unwanted leave; and the company should inform them that it will take care of any adverse results of the harassment. This may require actions such as crediting sick-leave banks for time taken off as a result of the harassment, giving extra time off, paying for counseling, reevaluating personal evaluations that could reflect bias, or any steps necessary to ensure that the harassed employees are put back in the position they would have been in had the harassment not occurred.

A vital part of any policy and procedures tells the workers what the possibilities are if they choose to violate the rules. Discipline should be quickly handed out once the investigation is complete, and should reflect both the severity of the incident and the perpetrator's history in this regard.

As the EEOC has stated, discipline should be designed to end the harassment and prevent the misconduct from occurring again. Often this will require not only handing out the appropriate discipline but also reminding the harasser that the policy provides for stricter penalties, up to and including dismissal, for continued misbehavior.

A policy should describe the disciplines that are possible and make clear that any discipline will be based on the individual situation, but could include dismissal. The policy should also state that further instances of harassing behavior after an employee has been found guilty of a violation of the policy will result in much more severe penalties. Specific examples should be given of possible discipline, whether it is dismissal, transfer of the harasser, a demotion, pay increase denials or pay reductions, adverse performance evaluations, or formal reprimands in the worker's file.

Many courts have found that a procedure that allows for merely asking the offending employee to stop the behavior is inadequate. If the policy has been clearly communicated to employees, such behavior should be viewed as breaking a company rule and treated accordingly. At a minimum, if the employer believes that a verbal reprimand is adequate because of the relatively minor content of the behavior, the harassed employee should be consulted as to her or his feelings on the matter. Do they think this is adequate? Why or why not?

Interestingly, at least one court has stated that, in certain situations, the mere presence of a harasser may create a hostile environment, and if transfer to another location is not possible, the harasser may have to be dismissed, even after a first offense. Each situation, including the past history of the harasser and the seriousness of the allegations, must be judged individually. It has been noted, for example, that "in some cases the mere presence of an employee who has engaged in particularly severe or pervasive harassment can create a hostile working environment."[3] The determination of what each situation requires can be made only by the investigator, and only after consultation with the complainant.

Consultation with the employee who has been harassed is vital with regard to any disciplinary decision. Studies show that most employees merely want the harassment to stop and the matter to be forgotten, rather than wanting revenge. They can be helpful in deciding how that can best be accomplished.

The case study policy merely states that an employee will be subject to appropriate sanctions. What does that term mean? The ambiguous wording is clearly inadequate, and the company needs to be more specific.

ADDITIONAL CONSIDERATIONS IN CARRYING OUT THE POLICY

Once a company has an adequate policy in effect, it must then carry it out in a manner that will further the chances for avoiding liability. Doing so will require procedures that take into consideration the special needs of the harassed employees and that seek to find out about and remedy problems before they can get out of hand.

Avoiding Solutions That Penalize Victims Once a complaint has been substantiated, an employer should take every precaution to ensure that it takes no actions that will work to the detriment of the employee who has been harassed. For example, any transfer of an employee who has been subjected to sexual harassment should only occur at the request of the employee herself or himself. The company should attempt to remedy any problems that may have resulted from the prohibited conduct and to include the affected employee in making decisions about actions taken in response to harassment.

Effective Communication of the Policy   Once it is put together, a company's policy must be clearly and regularly communicated to the employees. At the least, businesses should have their policies sent to all employees, posted in prominent locations throughout the workplace using graffiti-resistant paper for the posters, and pointed out to and included in any materials given to new employees. The responsibility for carrying out the policy must be made a part of the job description of anyone with authority in the workplace. If the poster is taken down, it should be replaced and an investigation undertaken to determine the source of the removal, as it may be an indication of a potential hostile environment problem already in existence. To be absolutely sure that the policy is being adequately communicated, it might be advisable to have employees (some companies do this only for new employees, although to be completely careful everyone should be included) sign a sheet that they have been given a copy of the policy and procedures and that they understand it. This signing should be done only after the employee is asked if there are any questions that he or she would like answered and should be done in a noncoercive manner, probably by the supervisor or head of personnel. Anyone who is going to be involved in presenting the policy and procedures to other employees should be carefully trained to do so in an appropriately serious manner and to answer any questions which might come up.

It is also a good idea for the policy to be accompanied by a letter from someone highly placed and respected in the company, preferably the CEO, expressing the company's serious commitment to the policy and to providing a workplace conducive to the success of all employees. It does not hurt for this letter to include an invitation to employees to approach the CEO (or whoever signs the letter for the company) if the employee feels that inadequate or inappropriate attention is being paid to complaints.

Compliance as Every Manager's Responsibility   Compliance with the policy and a managerial approach that pays close attention to the workplace environment should be required of all supervisory personnel. A manager's efforts with regard to ensuring a nondiscriminatory workplace and in investigating and dealing with situations that occur should be a well-known part of all managers' performance evaluations. It should be made clear to all managers that the company views broadly its managers' responsibility in this regard. Merely investigating complaints is inadequate. The manager should also make it his or her continual duty to know what is going on in the workplace and to personally handle any situations, whether reported or observed, that occur. This may include the responsibility to sensitively inquire as to the welcomeness of observed sexual advances, even if there is no outward indication of a problem. Of course, this also includes the duty to remove any and all demeaning materials and to make clear that they will not be tolerated.

The case study policy makes this important element clear. This is a strong point in its favor if it is challenged.

Affirmative Diagnostic Procedures   When an employee leaves a company, an exit interview is always a good idea. When it includes questions designed to find out about possible sexual harassment problems, it is an even better idea. Sensitively inquiring as to a person's reason for leaving the company, as well as about any problems that were not the cause of the employee's leaving, will help the company do a better job of controlling harassing behavior. Assuring the employee that reports of inappropriate conduct will not result in adverse consequences and will be subject to the same confidentiality any such complaint would receive (hopefully the program is so seriously conducted that this will not elicit laughter from the employee) will help in encouraging honest responses. If the exit interviewer is well trained, and the interviewee is really comfortable as to his or her protection, an employer may find out vital information and can deal with situations before they get out of hand.

If the interviewer finds that sexual harassment is the *cause* of the employee's exit, she or he should immediately alert the company, and every effort should be made to keep the employee from leaving, including offers of a different job location, adequate measures to halt the problem, and discipline of the offender. Some businesspeople are under the false assumption that if any employee voluntarily leaves, the company cannot be liable for damages caused by the sexual harassment. This is not the case. Under the doctrine of constructive discharge, employees can receive any or all of the remedies provided by law even if they resign, and in some states they have up to three years to bring a lawsuit. The courts feel that when conditions are intolerable, the situation should be viewed as if the employee was fired. This allows an award of back pay. Of course, attorney fees and pain and suffering damages may also be available.

In addition, when an employee reports that she or he is leaving because of sexual harassment, the company should reexamine its antiharassment program. Why did this employee not feel that the situation could be handled adequately while she or he was in the company's employ? Why did she or he feel it necessary to leave rather than report? This signals the possibility that the policy and procedures have flaws that might render them ineffective as defenses to a sexual harassment charge.

A business should not wait for people to leave before questioning them. Periodic questionnaires should be sent out promising confidentiality. Consideration should also be given to making the responses anonymous. A variety of questions should be asked that will help the company to perform better, but it is important to make sure that the questions are carefully designed to find out about harassment problems. It is not enough to ask, "Have you been sexually harassed in the workplace?" Many people would not label certain behavior as harassment (although programs should be helping them to do so). Instead, questions should be designed to elicit the necessary information, even if the person filling out the questionnaire does not understand the legal terminology. For example:

1. How comfortable are you in your workplace?
   a. Very comfortable
   b. Moderately comfortable
   c. Not very comfortable
   d. Very uncomfortable
2. What causes you stress on the job?
   a. Supervisor's unreasonable demands
   b. Co-workers' behavior
   c. Production demands
   d. Long hours

Carefully crafted surveys can be invaluable in searching out all sorts of work-force problems, especially in locating the source of potential sexual harassment situations.

The Payoff

Although putting together and carrying out an adequate anti–sexual harassment program will take some time and effort, the benefits with regard to lessening potential liability and increasing the morale of the workforce are extensive. In addition to quickly resolving any investigations by government agencies, businesses are finding that, even if cases are brought to court, judges are more open to quickly dismissing complaints when the defendant has followed the policy and procedure requirements carefully.

In the case of *Saxton v. American Telephone & Telegraph*,[4] for example, the lower court found it easy to dismiss the claim because of the company's process and its response to the woman's complaint. AT&T had a strong policy in effect, and it had begun an investigation the day after it was advised of the problem. A detailed report was completed within two weeks, and the perpetrator was transferred to another department within five weeks. The harassing employee, who had made unwelcome advances, was the complainant's supervisor. The court realized that the plaintiff had wanted even more in response, but it stated:

> No doubt from Saxton's perspective, AT&T could have done more to remedy the adverse effects of Richardson's conduct. But Title VII requires only that the

employer take steps reasonably likely to stop the harassment. . . . In another context, transfer of the wrongdoer to a different department might amount to an ineffectual slap on the wrist; but in this case, it served to terminate all contact between Richardson and Saxton and bring a definitive end to any harassment.[5]

Lawsuits by Fired Employees

Some recent cases have dealt with lawsuits by employees who have been discharged for sexual harassment. Many companies have made a commitment to fight the return of a harassing employee in court, if necessary, and are finding, on the whole, that courts are not sympathetic to such lawsuits. This is especially true if the employees knew about the penalties for violations of the sexual harassment policy, the investigation by the company was properly carried out, and the discipline was deemed appropriate in light of the seriousness of the conduct. Companies that make such a commitment and follow it up with actions should find that the workers are reassured about the seriousness of their employer's desire to ensure a comfortable work environment.

> *The case study policy, by not explicitly stating specific expected discipline, may be leaving the company open to lawsuits by any employee who is discharged for sexual harassment.*

Union Considerations

Another area of concern for unionized workplaces is the interplay of the contract, arbitration, and discipline for sexual harassment. Recently, a conflict has arisen in the lower courts over the handling of cases in which an arbitrator has ruled that dismissal of a union member for sexual harassment is unduly harsh and ordered the return of the offending employee. Some companies have gone to court requesting that the judge overturn the arbitrator's decision. Such a decision by a judge is, as any labor relations person knows, highly unusual. Courts usually give great deference to an arbitrator's decision, but in this circumstance, many of the federal appeals courts are more willing than usual to grant the employers' requests. In doing so, the courts are giving more weight to the public policy against sexual harassment than they are to their usual deference to a previous arbitration decision.

The Supreme Court has refused, so far, to accept a case that would finally decide this issue (it has denied appeals both in cases where the decision of the arbitrator was upheld and also where it was overturned). This leaves employers in a somewhat difficult position, but not one that is unworkable. Involving the union in formulating the company's policy and procedures and making these policy and procedures part of the contract will alleviate later problems. It is vital, however, that the company not bargain away the rights of employees to a policy and procedures that meets the EEOC requirements. Labor organizations are included in Title VII's antidiscrimination requirements, so they should also be willing to work with the employer in this regard to lessen their own potential for liability.

Summary

In conclusion, a legally adequate program for getting to the heart of sexual harassment problems in the workplace requires more than a general policy against the behavior. It requires the efforts and support of management at all levels and continual training of all workers, as well as a procedure that *encourages*—not merely *allows*—complaints. Once this process is in place, the business will not only be on strong footing in any legal action, but also find that the entire workforce benefits from an environment of cooperation and respect that can only reap benefits for the employer.

For Reflection

1. Discuss the difference between a policy that *allows* victims to come forward and one that *encourages* them.
2. Analyze why a separate sexual harassment policy is required.
3. Discuss some examples of types of behavior that could be viewed as sexual harassment and the discipline that would be appropriate for each.
4. Explain why it is important to explain the investigation procedures to employees.
5. Explain what the term *fail-safe* means with regard to a sexual harassment policy.

Notes

1. Meritor Savings Bank v. Vinson, 477 U.S. at 72.
2. Robinson v. Jacksonville Shipyards, 760 F. Supp. 1486 (M.D. Fla. 1991).
3. Ellison v. Brady, 924 F.2d at 883.
4. Saxton v. American Telephone & Telegraph, 10 F.3d 526 (7th Cir. 1993).
5. *Id.* at 536.

CHAPTER

Implementing Procedures for Resolving Complaints of Sexual Harassment

One of the questions that has been going through my mind that I started out with was some effort to reconcile the testimony of these two people who appear to be so credible.

—Senator Spector,
Senate Judiciary Confirmation Hearings
of Clarence Thomas, 1991

Introduction

In chapter 3 we introduced you to a case study that describes an employee's experience with a senior-level supervisor. This case study is reprinted here:

CASE STUDY

Mary has just arrived at her first job. Upon her arrival she is met by a supervisor who shows considerable interest in her work and experience in college. Mary is flattered by his interest and agrees to discuss her ideas

---

related to her work over lunch in a restaurant downtown. After a few lunches where the conversation is general and social rather than focused on professional issues, Mary finds that he is touching her—rubbing his knees against hers, placing his hand on her back and arms, and once patting her on the bottom. He asks Mary to meet him outside of work for early dinners. She declines, offering various excuses, and tries to maintain a polite but distant tone in her conversations with him. One day he asks Mary to come into his office to discuss a project. Once she is inside the office, he closes the door, moves toward her, and puts his arms around her. Mary tries to push him away, but he holds her tighter and tries to kiss her. There is a knock on the door, he releases Mary, and she opens the door and hurries out of the office.

In chapter 3 we asked you to decide whether sexual harassment occurred in this scenario. We also asked you to identify when in the account of Mary's experiences you believe sexual harassment occurred. Now, after rereading this case study, let's address Mary's experiences from her own perspective—not yours.

Consider the following addition to the scenario:

Three days after the occurrence in her supervisor's office, Mary makes an appointment to speak with you because she knows you are an investigator of sexual harassment complaints for your company.

How would you then answer the following questions?

1. What would you say when Mary comes into your office?
2. Where would you sit vis-à-vis Mary?
3. How would you answer the following questions she asks of you?
   a. What is sexual harassment?
   b. What did I do to encourage his behavior?
   c. Why did he do this to me?
   d. Am I naive?
   e. What can you do to help me?
   f. How many people here will know that I've come to talk with you?
   g. I'm not thinking too clearly. What information should I have so I can make a decision about what to do from here?
   h. Can you give me some suggestions about what I can do when I see him in the hall or in a meeting?
4. What would you do to end the meeting with Mary?

5. Mary phones you later in the week and tells you she's decided to file a formal complaint.
   a. What would you do next?
   b. After you've received her written complaint, what would you do?
   c. What would you say and do with the person complained about?
6. Outline the rest of the process you would follow.
7. The outcome is that the investigative team decided that sexual harassment had occurred and recommends a written reprimand.
   a. What do you and the investigative team do next?
   b. How will you communicate to Mary the outcome of the investigation?
   c. How will you communicate to the supervisor the outcome of the investigation?

None of these questions is easy to answer. In this chapter we will address each of the issues raised by the questions, for example, how to maintain confidentiality in the grievance process; how to interview witnesses, the complainant, and the accused; how to maintain records for your organization's purpose; and how to determine what sanctions to impose should a sexual harassment complaint be sustained. In the last chapter we discussed many of these issues from a legal perspective. In this chapter we will focus our discussion around the importance of the complaint procedures taking into account the psychological issues involved in the victimization process, including individuals' feelings of powerlessness, isolation, changes in social network patterns, and wish to gain control over their personal and professional lives. We begin with a discussion of the characteristics required of investigators of complaints of sexual harassment.

Who Should Investigate Complaints of Sexual Harassment

Each organization will select the individual who will be responsible for hearing and investigating charges of sexual harassment. At some companies, this role is usually given to the human resource department, affirmative action officer, or sexual harassment committees or panels. Conducting investigations of sexual harassment complaints requires two important requirements: sensitive, skilled individuals to conduct the grievance process and a supportive management.

Investigator Characteristics. Investigators must be aware that their presence at the organization is cause for discomfort for most employees. Sexual harassment is an uncomfortable issue for employees, as we have discussed throughout this text. By extension, individuals responsible for implementing sexual harassment policy statements, grievance procedures, and training programs make employees uncomfortable; these individuals are a constant reminder about the topic and about the organization's position statement.

Furthermore, no matter what the outcome of a grievance procedure, employees will be disappointed and even angry with the investigator. Investigators frequently get blamed for not doing enough work or for encouraging a "witch hunt." They thus must take comfort in knowing that they did their best in each complaint process.

The individuals who are responsible for investigating complaints should meet the following criteria that have been identified by psychologists and human resource specialists.[1] They must

1. have sufficient credibility in the area of sexual harassment, including knowledge and formal training in the legal, psychological, and physical aspects of sexual harassment;
2. be readily accessible for employees and administrators;
3. have skill in relating to people and eliciting information from them;
4. not be uncomfortable in discussing matters of sexuality and sexual deviancy, incest, battering, and rape;
5. be fluent in languages in addition to English;
6. report directly to the individual who will determine the company's response (i.e., administer sanctions);
7. not permit any of the individuals in the complaint procedure to pressure them to reveal confidential information, to become their advocate, or to take sides in the final report of the investigation;
8. be honest and candid, without permitting personal feelings to interfere with effectiveness;
9. be sensitive to civil-service rules, collective bargaining agreements, and other personnel rules;
10. be prepared for discussions to be very emotional, and be prepared to be a calming force for these emotional discussions;
11. set up a safe atmosphere for the complainant, alleged harasser, and witnesses to discuss their perspectives without the fear of being ridiculed or judged;
12. maintain a distance from all individuals involved in the complaint process so that (a) a reasoned judgment can be made about whether to sustain the charge of sexual harassment and (b) the investigator can be upheld as objective by individuals such as hearing officers, judges, and parties involved in the complaint process;
13. not use tape recorders or video recorders during interviews as part of the investigative process because these machines create unnecessary added stress for individuals;
14. ask parties not to discuss the complaint with others (this is essential to lessen the probability of retaliation and influence other witnesses);
15. know that the organization has a legal, as well as an ethical, obligation to make the workplace an environment free of sexual harassment and free of the fear of retaliation for speaking about sexual harassment;
16. work well with the president and not be viewed as adversarial.

We recommend *behavioral rehearsal techniques* (see exhibit 5.1) for investigators to practice nonverbal as well as verbal communication. As is

EXHIBIT 5.1

Behavioral Rehearsal of Verbal and Nonverbal Communication

When making general statements about women (or any other group), be sure that the statements are based on accurate information, not on stereotypes.

Avoid humor or gratuitous remarks that demean or belittle people because of their sex, sexual orientation, race, religion, or physical characteristics.

Avoid using generic masculine terms to refer to people of both sexes. Although the effort to do this may involve some initial discomfort, it will result in more precise communication and understanding.

When using illustrative examples, avoid stereotypes, such as making all victims of sexual harassment women and all harassers men.

Try to monitor your behavior toward women and men. For example:

Do you give more time to men than to women?

Do you treat men more seriously than women?

Are you systematically more attentive to questions, observations, and responses made by women victims than by men victims?

Do you direct more of your own questions, observations and responses to individuals of one sex?

Do you assume a heterosexual model when referring to human behavior?

Do you maintain eye contact when you are listening to individuals involved in a complaint procedure? Or do you shift your gaze away from them?

Are you someone who smiles even when hearing sad or discomforting information? An employee may interpret your smiling to mean that you believe her or his complaint or position on sexual harassment is silly or is without merit.

Do you let people know you are listening to them? Do you nod and say "hm hm"? How do you convey your interest and concern?

Adapted from M.A. Paludi and R.B. Barickman, Academic and Workplace Sexual Harassment: A Resource Manual (Albany: State University of New York Press, 1991). By permission of the State University of New York Press. © 1991.

indicated in exhibit 5.1, this rehearsal must include being in tune with other individuals' psychological responses to sexual harassment.

Management Characteristics. Management must support its investigators of complaints of sexual harassment. Management must give its investigators the autonomy and power they require to undertake an effective investigation. It can't ignore the knowledge of a sexual harassing situation, even if no complaint has been filed, and should never tell investigators to quash a complaint or find in favor of the accused or the complainant. Simply, management must stay out of the way of an investigation until it is needed to institute sanctions (to be discussed later in this chapter). No retaliation against the investigator must be exhibited. Should an investigator experience an unresponsive or hostile management, we recommend the investigator seek new employment.

Women or Men as Investigators

It is common for investigators to report gender comparisons in employees discussing their sexual harassment experiences with them. For example, men may be more comfortable talking with women investigators. This is especially the case when the men have been sexually harassed by other men. Women may be reluctant to discuss their experiences with a male investigator because of the sometimes explicitly sexual nature of many complaints of sexual harassment. We thus recommend having a team of investigators—both a woman and a man.

The team of investigators can rely on each other for support. For women complainants, the team approach offers a safer environment than talking about sexuality with an unknown man. It is also important to have a second investigator should a complaint be filed against the other. In this case, the complainant will have an opportunity to file a complaint at the organization. Without two investigators, the complainant has no option. Of course, if the complainant files against one member of the investigative team, the accused must exclude herself or himself from the investigatory process.

Psychological Issues Involved in the Victimization Process: Making Them Central to the Investigatory Process

As we pointed out in chapter 3, research has suggested that individuals who experience sexual harassment frequently exhibit the following responses to sexual harassment:

> Confusion and/or embarrassment
> > Am I overreacting? Have I misinterpreted the situation?
> > Have I done something to lead him/her on?

Helplessness

> No one is going to believe me. It's his or her word against mine.
> If I complain, it will make matters worse.

Anger

> I'm being cheated out of a job. Why isn't anyone doing something about his or her behavior?

Worry

> I'll never get a good recommendation from him or her if I don't go along with him or her. All the other managers will know if I file a complaint. Everyone will say I'm too sensitive.

These responses center around individuals' feelings of having no control over the situation. This is especially true because of the humiliating and disorienting impact of sexual harassment, where the victim may experience the sort of self-doubt, self-blame, and sense of degradation common to victims of rape, incest, and battering. It is important, therefore, that the means of hearing and resolving complaints of sexual harassment take into account individuals' psychological responses and offer a grievance procedure that will ease the burden of discussing their experiences. Unless employees feel they will have this protection of confidentiality, they will seldom report the sexual harassment they have experienced. And, of course, individual complaints cannot be resolved, and the pervasive injury done to the organization by sexual harassment cannot be remedied unless complaints are actually reported.

We therefore recommend that the investigative process take into consideration the emotional responses to sexual harassment to assist the complainant's path to recovery from the trauma of sexual harassment. For example:

Complainant's Response: Confusion

Investigator's Response: Help with labelling of experiences, provide behavioral definitions of sexual harassment

Complainant's Response: Helplessness

Investigator's Response: Discuss complainant's power in handling case, focus on ways individual is powerful in other aspects of her or his life

Complainant's Response: Anger

Investigator's Response: Discuss confidentiality of investigative process; focus on ways to rebuild career; offer support systems

Complainant's Response: Worry

Investigator's Response: Discuss due process, sanctions against retaliation, confidentiality of investigative process

Research has documented that the experience of participating in an investigative process is as emotionally and physically stressful as the victimization itself. It is important to build in several support systems to help complainants and alleged harassers cope with the process of the complaint procedure. Investigators who must make a determination whether to sustain the complaint must not also be a counselor to either party who clearly needs support during the complaint process. Referrals for support groups and therapists in the community must be made readily available for complainants and alleged harassers.

Part of an Employees Assistance Program (EAP) in an organization may be devoted to dealing with individuals involved in a sexual harassment complaint procedure. Counselors in an EAP must be trained in the psychological issues involved in sexual harassment. It is important not to convey too early to any of the individuals involved in an investigation that they are perceived to be in need of psychological help. Complainants, for example, may interpret such a referral as the investigator telling them they are "crazy" and that they "made up" the whole experience. A sample handout for these purposes is presented in exhibit 5.2.

Supportive Techniques for Working with Individuals Involved in a Sexual Harassment Investigatory Process

All individuals involved in an investigation of a sexual harassment complaint must be treated sensitively in the investigatory process. Counselors, peer support staff, and Employee Assistance Program workers must offer the following supportive techniques to the complainant, accused, and witnesses:

1. Acknowledge individuals' courage by stating how difficult it is to label, report, and discuss sexual harassment.
2. Encourage individuals to share their feelings and perceptions.
3. Provide information about the incidence of sexual harassment. Also share the symptoms associated with Sexual Harassment Trauma Syndrome.
4. Assure complainants that they are not responsible for their victimization.
5. Work with individuals in their search for the meaning in their victimization; support them while they mourn their losses.
6. Work with individuals in monitoring their physical, emotional, and interpersonal responses to sexual harassment and to the investigatory process.
7. Provide a safe forum for individuals' expression of anger and resentment.
8. Work with individuals on ways to validate themselves so as to feel empowered.
9. Suggest a peer counseling group for individuals who need support for dealing with their experiences. See exhibit 5.3 for information about support groups on sexual harassment.
10. Work with individuals and the organization in their investigation of complaints of sexual harassment.

EXHIBIT 5.2

Referrals for Therapeutic Support

Many individuals who have participated in an investigation of a sexual harassment complaint have reported that they wanted some neutral party to be a sounding board for them, someone to help them sort out all the emotions they were experiencing during the investigatory process.

We at _____ (name of organization) have prepared the following list of therapeutic support systems for individuals who are involved in an investigation of sexual harassment. We have prepared this list to serve as a reference guide for individuals and support groups who may be contacted by employees here at _____.

We have also presented some national organizations from which employees may request written information concerning sexual harassment in general and therapeutic support in particular.

National Organizations

9 to 5
614 Superior Avenue, NW
Cleveland, OH 44113
800-522-0925

Coalition of Labor Union Women
15 Union Square
New York, NY 10003
212-242-0700

National Council for
   Research on Women
The Sara Delano Roosevelt
   Memorial House
47-49 East 65th Street
New York, NY 10021
212-570-5001

Women Employed
22 West Monroe
Suite 1400
Chicago, IL 60603

Equal Rights Advocates
1663 Mission Street
Suite 550
San Francisco, CA 94103
415-621-0672

Federally Employed Women
1400 I Street NW
Washington, DC 20005
202-898-0994

NOW Legal Defense Fund
9 Hudson Street
New York, NY 10013
212-925-6635

Women's Legal Defense Fund
1875 Connecticut Avenue, NW
Washington, DC 20009
202-986-2600

Local Organizations

. . .

EXHIBIT 5.3

Suggestions for Support Groups on Sexual Harassment

GOALS

Listen to and respect individuals' reactions to being sexually harassed.

Sort out sound choices with respect to dealing with sexual harassment.

Be aware of the commonality of themes in group members' lives.

Define *quid pro quo* and hostile environment sexual harassment.

Discuss psychological issues involved in dealing with sexual harassment.

Discuss the physical and emotional reactions to being sexually harassed.

Provide a psychological profile of sexual harassers.

Discuss peer sexual harassment.

Discuss means of resolution for complaints of sexual harassment.

Assess our own perceptions of the definition, incidence, and psychological dimensions of sexual harassment.

RESPONSIBILITIES

Support-group members agree to avoid judging and to focus on giving support and making positive statements to each person, even when making a difficult comment.

Time arrangements (both beginning and end) are agreed upon and honored by all members.

Any confrontation is clear, gentle, and nurturing.

Members agree to come every time unless it is impossible to do so.

Confidential information must never be relayed to others outside a support group.

Privacy must be respected at all times.

An atmosphere of safety and security must be maintained at all times.

Each individual has the responsibility of taking care of herself or himself.

Therapists must know that they may be asked to provide information regarding their treatment of an individual involved in an investigatory process. Victims of sexual harassment suffer long-term aftereffects because (1) sexual harassment is a trauma; (2) sexual harassment is a violation of trust, especially when the harasser is in a position of authority; and (3) sexual harassment causes secondary losses, including the lack of support and comfort from family and friends and retaliation because of filing charges (e.g., being fired).[2]

It is important that the therapist understand that his or her role is not to judge whether sexual harassment as legally defined has occurred. In addition, the support system is not an attorney. Counselors must only help individuals with their options, not advise them on their civil rights. Understanding the psychological impact of sexual harassment must include an awareness that the victim's perceptions and cognitive appraisals of her or his experiences activates negative self-images. Frequently, victims of sexual harassment view themselves as needy, frightened, weak, and out of control. For the victimization caused by sexual harassment to be resolved, shattered beliefs must be reformulated to assimilate the experience of sexual harassment. This process has been termed *cognitive readjustment*.[3] Successful cognitive readjustment of beliefs includes a discovered ability to cope, learn, adapt, and become self-reliant. Cognitive readjustment produces a greater sense of self-confidence, maturity, honesty, and sense of strength.

Responding to a Complaint of Sexual Harassment

Allegations of sexual harassment are accompanied by decreased productivity in the workplace, morale problems among employees, adverse publicity, and perhaps the filing of EEOC charges. It is most important, therefore, to treat sexual harassment complaints seriously and sensitively. Furthermore, we recommend that investigators follow a consistent plan for all complaints of sexual harassment. This plan includes the following stages for formal complaints that are filed in the workplace:

1. Prepare the materials needed for a formal complaint procedure.
2. Review the legal and psychological issues involved in sexual harassment in general and investigatory procedures specifically.
3. Identify all information the complainant will have to address in the formal complaint.
4. Investigate the complaint filed.
5. Prepare a report of the investigation.
6. Discuss the investigation with the president or CEO.
7. Assist the president or CEO with possible recommendations for remedial action.
8. Institute remedial action and write a response to all parties involved in the investigatory process.

Each of these steps is described in detail in the following section.

Prepare the materials needed for a formal complaint procedure. The materials needed for conducting a formal investigation are the following:

1. standard notification form for complainant
2. standard notification form for accused
3. standard notification forms for witnesses
4. standard note-taking form

Examples of each notification form are presented in exhibit 5.4. These forms must be prepared on the company's stationary. Copies should be sent via certified mail to all parties involved in the investigation. We recommend that notification letters should be sent to the individuals' home address, not work address.

EXHIBIT 5.4

Standard Notification Forms

EXAMPLE OF STANDARD NOTIFICATION LETTER FOR WITNESSES

Date

Name
Home Address

Dear ___ :

I am writing to inform you that I was given your name by ___ (either complainant or accused) to contact you regarding being a witness in a sexual harassment complaint filed by ___ against ___. This is in following the investigative procedures of sexual harassment at (name of organization).

In accordance with these procedures, I would like to meet with you in person to discuss your evidence. I am available to meet with you at one of the following times: ___. Will you please call me this week to set up a meeting time? Or, if you wish, you may leave a message for me at ___ . You may write to me in care of ___.

Your name or other identifying information will not be made known to ___. I have enclosed a copy of our policy statement and procedures.

Sincerely,

_____

Sexual Harassment Investigator

EXHIBIT 5.4, continued

Standard Notification Forms

EXAMPLE OF STANDARD NOTIFICATION LETTER FOR COMPLAINANT

Date

Name
Home Address

Dear _____:

I am writing to inform you that I am in receipt of your written formal complaint of sexual harassment against _____, under the procedures of sexual harassment at _____ (name of organization).

In accordance with these procedures, I would like to meet with you to discuss your complaint. I am available to meet with you at one of the following times: _____. Will you please call me this week to set up a meeting time? Or, if you wish, you may leave a message for me at _____. You may write to me in care of _____.

I am interested in resolving this matter as quickly as possible. Our first priority will be to attempt to resolve the problem through a mutual agreement of the complainant and the person complained against. I have enclosed another copy of our policy statement and procedures.

Sincerely,

_____

Sexual Harassment Investigator

Review the legal and psychological issues involved in sexual harassment in general and investigatory procedures specifically. We recommend a review of the following materials:

1. legal definition of sexual harassment
2. interviewing techniques for use with complainant and accused
3. Sexual Harassment Trauma Syndrome symptoms
4. suggested questions to ask during interviews

EXHIBIT 5.4, continued

Standard Notification Forms

EXAMPLE OF STANDARD NOTIFICATION LETTER
FOR ACCUSED

Date

Name
Home Address

Dear _____:

I am writing to inform you that I am in receipt of a formal complaint of sexual harassment against you made by _____, under the procedures of sexual harassment at _____ (name of organization).

In accordance with these procedures, I would like to meet with you to discuss the complaint and your responses to it. I am available to meet with you at one of the following times: _____. Will you please call me this week to set up a meeting time? Or, if you wish, you may leave a message for me at _____. You may write to me in care of _____.

I am of course, interested in resolving this matter as quickly as possible. Our first priority will be to attempt to resolve the problem through a mutual agreement of the complainant and the person complained against. I have enclosed another copy of our policy statement and procedures. In addition, I have enclosed a copy of_____'s formal complaint.

I welcome any questions you have about the policy and procedures and will be pleased to discuss them with you when you contact me to set up an appointment.

Sincerely,

_____
Sexual Harassment Investigator

A summary of resources for this review is presented in exhibit 5.5. In addition, we recommend the review of chapters 2 and 3 in this book for the legal and psychological issues involved in sexual harassment.

EXHIBIT 5.5

Resources for Investigators

LEGAL ISSUES OF SEXUAL HARASSMENT

Connell, Dana. "Effective Sexual Harassment Policies: Unexpected Lessons from Jacksonville Shipyards." *Employee Relations* 17 (1991): 191–206.
EEOC Policy Guidance on Sexual Harassment (March 1990).
Shattuck, Cathie, and Kathleen Williams. *Employer's Guide to Controlling Sexual Harassment.* Washington: Thompson Publishing Group, 1992.
Solotoff, Lawrence, and Henry Kramer. *Sex Discrimination and Sexual Harassment in the Workplace.* New York: Law Journal Seminars Press, 1994.

PSYCHOLOGICAL ISSUES OF SEXUAL HARASSMENT

Fitzgerald, Louise F. "Sexual Harassment: Violence against Women in the Workplace." *American Psychologist* 48 (1993): 1070–76.
Gutek, Barbara, and Mary Koss. "Changed Women and Changed Organizations: Consequences of and Coping with Sexual Harassment." *Journal of Vocational Behavior* 42 (1993): 28–48.
Rabinowitz, Vita C. "Coping with Sexual Harassment." In *Ivory Power: Sexual Harassment on Campus,* edited by M. Paludi. Albany: State University of New York Press, 1990.

Identify all information the complainant will have to address in the formal complaint. The content of a formal complaint of sexual harassment should include the following components:

Part 1: Information concerning verbal and/or nonverbal behavior; dates, time, witnesses present
Part 2: How complainant felt and still feels; impact on work performance
Part 3: What complainant wants for resolution of complaint

The complaint must be signed, dated, and addressed to the sexual harassment investigator, care of the investigator working with the complainant.

Investigate the complaint filed. We recommend the following process for investigators to follow from the time a written formal complaint has been received:

1. Send standard notification letter to complainant via certified mail to her or his home address.

2. Send standard notification letter to accused via certified mail to his or her home address. With this notification letter also send

   copy of complaint

   copy of organization's policy statement and grievance procedures.

3. Notify the president or CEO about the formal complaint received and investigation pending. Start file of correspondence for the president/CEO, as well as for investigators.

4. Use standard note-taking form for meetings with complainant and accused (see exhibit 5.6 for a sample note-taking form). Complete the information following the meeting because it is distracting to the individuals involved to have the in-

---

EXHIBIT 5.6

Note-Taking Form

Date of meeting or call: _____

Individual's name: _____

Telephone numbers: _____

Description of sexual harassment problem (nature of incident, time, dates, description of alleged harasser, health- and work-related consequences):

Symptom checklist (please ask individual whether or not the following symptoms have been experienced since the harassment started. Circle or check off those experienced.)

Career Effects
- Changes in work habits
- Drop in work performance because of stress
- Absenteeism
- Withdrawal from work
- Changes in career goals

Physical Reactions
- Headaches
- Inability to concentrate
- Sleep disturbances
- Lethargy
- Gastrointestinal distress

Changes in Self-Perception
- Poor self-concept or self-esteem
- Powerlessness
- Isolation
- Lack of competency

Emotional Reactions
- Shock, denial
- Anger, frustration
- Guilt
- Shame, powerlessness
- Insecurity, embarrassment

- Respiratory problems
- Phobias, panic reactions
- Nightmares
- Eating disorders
- Dermatological reactions

Social Effects
- Withdrawal
- Fear of new people
- Lack of trust
- Change in physical appearance
- Change in social networks

Other Symptoms:

Additional critical facts:

Verbal objection:

Written objection:

Consultation with therapist or support group:

Consultation with physician:

Date of receipt of written complaint:

Date of notification of receipt of complaint:

Date of notification of alleged harasser:

Date of meeting(s) with alleged harasser:

Outcome of meeting:

Outcome of subsequent meetings with complainant:

Date of meeting(s) with witnesses:

Follow-up contacts:

Date: Who called: Content:

vestigator constantly with her or his head lowered and taking notes. Investigators must respond to the individuals physically as well as psychologically. Sample questions to be asked of both parties are presented in exhibit 5.7.

5. Use standard notification letters for witnesses for each party. Send the letter via certified mail to the witnesses' home addresses.

6. Notify parties involved that witnesses have been contacted. The identity of the witnesses should not be disclosed in this correspondence.

7. Review any correspondence sent between the parties involved in the investigation. Where necessary, and with permission from the individual involved in the investigation, review any company files (e.g., supervisor's performance evaluations, etc.).

EXHIBIT 5.7

Questions to Ask During Interviews

WITH COMPLAINANT

Tell me what happened that made you decide to come see me.

What specifically was said, done to you, etc.?

When did this behavior occur—date, time, etc.?

How did this behavior make you feel?

Did you or are you now experiencing any of the following symptoms after this incident occurred? (Show Sexual Harassment Trauma Syndrome symptoms)

Tell me what you want the sexual harassment committee to do to help you with the issue you told me about today.

WITH ACCUSED

Now that you've had an opportunity to review the complaint, tell me about your perspective on the incidents described in the report.

The behaviors described in this report are unacceptable here. Do you know that?

How did you think your comments/touch (fill in the behavior) made ___ (the complainant) feel?

Were you surprised by what _____ (the complainant) said about how your behavior impacted on her/him?

WITH WITNESSES

Tell me what you observed with respect to the incident under investigation.

What did the people involved say or do?

Prepare a report of the investigation. A report of the investigation should be prepared directly from the note-taking form used throughout the entire investigation. This report should include the findings of the allegation and the following decisions made by the investigator:

Should the complaint be sustained?

If no, this information and the reasons believed to substantiate this decision must be explained.

If yes, this information and the reasons for the decision and recommendations for corrective action must be identified.

If the investigator believes there is insufficient information on which to offer an answer to this question, we recommend that the investigator interview parties again, following the procedures that have been outlined here.

Discuss the investigation with the president or CEO.

Assist the president or CEO with recommendations for remedial action.

Institute remedial action and write a response to all parties involved in the investigatory process. Send a copy of this full report to the president; keep a copy in your office for the time being. No other copies should be kept from this point on. The president will now have to initiate corrective action. Letters should be sent from the president's office concerning the outcome of the investigation to all individuals—complainant, accused, and witnesses.

Types of sanctions include the following:

Verbal and/or written reprimands concerning the harasser's behavior and how the workplace will not tolerate any further behavior of this type. Written reprimands may be placed in the individual's personnel file. These reprimands must also make clear that further complaints will result in more severe sanctions, including dismissal.

Dismissal when more severe sexual harassment has occurred. Should the president accept this recommendation from the investigator, then collective bargaining agreements procedures must be followed. Investigators should be used as expert witnesses in any subsequent hearings related to the charges of sexual harassment against an employee.

Suspension may be an option when the recommendation involves counseling or other rehabilitative processes. This suspension should not be viewed as a reward; the suspension must not include paid salary.

Transfers for one or both individuals to other positions within the workplace may be appropriate. This type of remedial action helps with potential retaliation.

Demotions of supervisory employees to nonsupervisory positions may be a sanction that is considered prior to suspension or dismissal.

Requiring attendance at a sexual harassment training program.

Apologizing to the victim.

Should a complaint be determined to be totally fabricated, the organization may want to take steps to restore the reputation of the accused if she or he was damaged by the proceedings. Such steps may include a statement read at a manager's meeting or note in a newsletter or other appropriate action.

From the Laboratory to the Real World

As a summary of the procedures we recommend be followed for conducting a formal investigation of sexual harassment, let us return to the case study involving Mary and her supervisor. (You may want to reread the case study at the beginning of this chapter.)

We asked you to consider that Mary makes an appointment to speak with you in your role as an investigator of sexual harassment complaints. We now offer some suggested responses to the questions posed at the beginning of the chapter. We invite you to compare our responses to the ones you gave.

What would you say when Mary comes into your office?

Thank her for coming.

Acknowledge the difficulty in coming to speak with an investigator.

Explain that your role in this first meeting is to listen to her and work with her in identifying her concerns.

Where would you sit vis-à-vis Mary?

Ask Mary to choose between two seats—one across from you, the other next to you. Recall the importance of putting control into individuals' lives.

How would you answer the following questions she asks of you?

What is sexual harassment?

Provide behavioral examples of sexual harassment.

Then fill in with legal terms (e.g., *hostile environment*)

Show Mary the handout you will give to her with all of the terms and examples clearly defined.

What did I do to encourage his behavior?

Explain that behaviors on the part of others may not be elicited.

Indicate it is common to blame oneself when these things happen.

Why did he do this to me? Am I naive?

Suggest that individuals who engage in this type of behavior often do so with a variety of people. Mary probably wasn't singled out because she was naive, attractive, single, or other such reasons.

Tell her that since she was relatively new to the company and didn't know the politics of the place yet, she might have been targeted for the behavior.

What can you do to help me?

Discuss the policy statement and grievance procedures.

Highlight the points you are making on the materials for Mary to keep.

Review the procedures at least three times.

Remind Mary that it is entirely her choice to file a complaint.

Alert Mary to your legal obligation to investigate a complaint when a situation is brought to your attention, even if the individual does not wish to file a complaint.

How many people here will know that I've come to talk with you?

For a formal complaint, only the investigator and the president will know.

I'm not thinking too clearly. What information should I have so I can make a decision about what to do from here?

Discuss the policy statement and grievance procedures step by step.

Can you give me some suggestions about what I can do when I see him in the hall or in a meeting?

Tell Mary she doesn't have to talk with the supervisor. She can leave the situation if she can. If she feels she has no choice but to say something—like hello—tell Mary she can get by with the minimum conversation. Tell Mary to report any incident to you.

Engage in some behavioral rehearsal with Mary; take turns playing both roles.

What would you do to end the meeting with Mary?

Remind Mary about her choices. Tell her you are obligated to investigate once the matter is brought to your attention.

Thank her again for coming to talk with you. Set up another meeting with Mary prior to her leaving. Be sure Mary has your phone number.

Mary phones you later in the week and tells you she's decided to file a formal complaint. What would you do next?

Remind Mary about the three parts to a formal complaint: (1) what was done and said, (2) how she feels, and (3) what she wants to happen.

Ask Mary to address the complaint to you as the investigator.

After you've received her written complaint, what would you do?

Send Mary the standard notification form for complainants.

Send the supervisor the appropriate standard notification form.

Alert the president that there is a formal complaint under investigation.

Meet with Mary and the supervisor individually.

If there are witnesses, use standard notification forms to notify them; interview them.

The outcome is that the investigative team decided that sexual harassment had occurred and recommends a written reprimand. What do you do next?

Prepare a full report of the investigation, including your suggestions for corrective action.

Give this report to the President.

How will you communicate with Mary the outcome of the investigation?

Send a letter to Mary telling her that the investigation is completed and that she will be hearing from the president shortly.

Put letter in file for the president.

How will you communicate with the supervisor about the outcome of the investigation?

Send a letter to the supervisor telling him that the investigation is completed and that he will be hearing from the president shortly.

Put letter in file for the president.

Informal Complaints of Sexual Harassment

Using a formal complaint procedure can be intimidating to individuals. These procedures take time and can cause considerable embarrassment and stress for all those involved in the process. We recommend providing individuals with an option of filing an informal complaint of sexual harassment in addition to the formal procedures we outlined above.

If the individual bringing the complaint is willing to be identified to the person against whom the complaint is made and wishes to attempt informal resolution of the problem, the investigator will make a confidential record of the circumstances (signed by the complainant) and undertake appropriate discussions with the person or people involved.

This type of complaint procedure works best with types of hostile environment sexual harassment, especially gender harassment (see chapter 3). Should complainants not be satisfied with the outcome of the informal procedure, they should be provided the option of using the formal complaint process; the steps to follow would be identical to those discussed above. Organizations cannot take disciplinary action using informal procedures; disciplinary action requires a formal complaint. Informal complaints are aimed at stopping the behavior in an immediate way rather than determining culpability or intent.

Record keeping of informal complaint procedures must be adequately maintained in order to determine whether the same offender may be part of several informal resolutions.

Mediation as a Procedure for Resolving Complaints of Sexual Harassment

In recent years, some institutions have built into their grievance procedures a mediation technique, whereby grievances can be resolved informally between the individuals involved. In a mediation procedure, the complainant and accused typically meet together with a mediator to attempt to resolve the sexual harassment. In this session, both parties tell their side of the story to the mediator in the presence of the other party. It has been proposed that employees may prefer mediation to a formal complaint process for the follow-ing reasons: faster resolution, preservation of confidentiality, and avoiding the stress of a formal process. However, such sessions very often become volatile. Individuals have very powerful emotions associated with the situa-tion. Furthermore, such a procedure assumes both individuals are of equal power in the organization. Research has suggested, however, that most vic-tims of sexual harassment hold less organizational power than the harassers. Perhaps most importantly, most individuals who have experienced sexual harassment want to flee the harasser, not sit with this person face-to-face. They fear the mediation session will become an extension of the sexual ha-rassment.

We thus recommend against mediation as a technique for resolving complaints of sexual harassment. In the informal complaint process we dis-cussed above, the investigator does serve as a mediator. However, this inves-tigator will listen to each party individually and summarize their statements for the other party. The parties never meet face-to-face.

Additional Issues in Investigating Complaints of Sexual Harassment

Individuals may be unable to file a formal complaint of sexual harassment within a short time frame following their experiences. They may not want to take this assertive response (see chapter 3) or they may be worried about a pending performance appraisal and possible retaliation. The statute for limita-tions should therefore not be too restrictive. We recommend sixty days from realization of the discomfort of the situation. For individuals who wish to file a complaint, but hold off for a few weeks until the investigation begins (e.g., because they have a performance review scheduled), this request must be granted by the investigator.

Informal complaints of sexual harassment can usually be dealt with within a couple of days of the investigator's hearing about the situation. For-mal complaints can take much longer, depending on the schedule of individu-als involved, the number of witnesses involved, and other factors. Because the grievance procedure is an emotionally laden process, we recommend con-ducting the investigation within a two-week time period, not to exceed one month from receipt of the formal complaint. This time frame must be articu-lated to all parties involved in the grievance procedure; it will help provide a sense of closure to them.

Closure must also be provided at the completion of the investigation with a letter of apology sent to the complainant from the president or CEO should the complaint be sustained.

Summary

Whereas each business will set up a complaint procedure that fits the unique needs of that business, the following general guidelines we have identified in this chapter should apply for all investigations of sexual harassment:

1. Clearly state to all parties involved in the investigative procedure that the company has an obligation to maintain a workplace free of sexual harassment and free of the fear of being retaliated against for filing a complaint of sexual harassment. Investigators must also state that they cannot ignore any complaint of sexual harassment.

2. Take every complaint seriously.

3. Keep every complaint confidential. The need for confidentiality is essential to protect the rights of those who filed the complaint, those against whom the complaint has been filed, and witnesses.

4. Do not make any conclusions about the veracity of the complaint until the investigation is completed. Investigators must not make determinations about the complaint based on the reputations of the individuals involved.

5. The investigation must be thorough and fair. The workplace's policy statement and procedures must be followed at all times. There must be provisions, for example, for hearing complaints against the investigator. New procedures must not be developed during the course of an investigation.

6. Document every step of the investigation completely and accurately in a form that can be defended to others. This procedure should be maintained for the in-house investigation and for subsequent lawsuits, for which all notes, reports, and written materials will be subpoenaed and be made part of the court record.

7. Complete investigations in a timely fashion. A prompt investigation is necessary to obtain accurate and complete statements from all individuals involved in the complaint. A quick time frame also assists in the complainant's coping with the victimization. Time deadlines for individuals to respond to charges of sexual harassment must be rigorously observed.

8. Interview the complainant in detail. The following information must be obtained from the complainant in writing:

   detailed description of the behavior about which the individual is complaining (i.e., approximate dates, times, frequency, location, circumstances, identity of alleged harasser)

   names of potential witnesses

   impact of behavior on complainant in terms of emotional, physical, or work productivity

   whether individual has voiced her or his concern to alleged harasser and, if so, the outcome of such objection

   the type of resolution the individual is seeking for herself or himself and for the alleged harasser.

9. Interview the person complained about in detail. The person must be shown the written complaint and documents given to the investigator. The following information must be obtained in writing from the individual against whom the complaint was filed:

   reaction to complaint

   interpretation of events mentioned in complaint

   understanding of the impact of his or her behavior on complainant

10. Interview all witnesses. Witnesses identified by the complainant and by the alleged harasser should be invited to meet with the investigator. Witnesses should discuss only information related to the incidents about which they are assumed to have knowledge with respect to the complaint at hand. They must not be interviewed about information they have about previous victims, for example. The identity of the witnesses for the complainant must not be provided for the alleged harasser. Similarly, the identity of the witnesses for the alleged harasser must not be given to the complainant. This confidentiality will ensure that witnesses will come forth and participate in the investigative process without fear of retaliation.

11. Review all documents presented by the complainant, alleged harasser, and witnesses. Documents include, but are not limited to, performance appraisals, letters, and notes sent to an individual involved in the complaint process. Investigators must not seek out any additional records without the prior written consent from the individual(s) involved, and only when these materials are deemed absolutely necessary to conduct the investigation.

12. Handle each complaint against the same individual independently. The outcome of the investigation should never be based on knowledge that the alleged harasser has had other complaints filed against him or her. Similarly, knowledge that the complainant has filed other complaints must not enter into the investigative process. Such information may be helpful in determining sanctions, however.

13. Make provisions for individuals who wish to wait until they receive a performance appraisal prior to filing a complaint. This need may be met by instituting an anonymous complaint procedure whereby individuals do not have to sign their name to the complaint in order for it to be investigated. This complaint procedure works best when one or several employees file a complaint against a manager. Another way to meet this need is to provide more lenient time frames for filing complaints, for example, not five days or two weeks when one month would be better for the complainant.

14. Provide closure for all parties involved in the complaint procedure. Information regarding the status of the investigation and the completion of the investigation must be provided to all individuals involved in the complaint process. Contact the complainant periodically for at least one year to determine whether the resolution of the complaint is satisfactory, whether she or he has experienced any retaliation, and whether there has been any recurrence of the sexual harassment. The individual who has engaged in sexual harassment should also be contacted periodically for one year to determine whether the investigator can provide any subsequent assistance, such as referrals for therapeutic support.

For Reflection

1. Identify the reasons why grievance procedures are important in dealing with sexual harassment in any organization.
2. Identify several characteristics of a good investigator of sexual harassment complaints.
3. Outline the responsibilities of management with respect to empowering its investigators.
4. What are the benefits to having both a woman and man as a team of investigators?
5. Give an example of relating the grievance procedure to a psychological response of being victimized by sexual harassment.
6. Discuss ways therapeutic support can be beneficial to individuals who are going through a grievance procedure.
7. Identify the steps investigators should take to deal with a formal complaint of sexual harassment.
8. Distinguish between an informal and a formal complaint of sexual harassment.
9. Offer some objections for using mediation as a technique in the grievance process.

Notes

1. M. A. PALUDI & R. B. BARICKMAN, ACADEMIC AND WORKPLACE SEXUAL HARASSMENT: A MANUAL OF RESOURCES (1991). H. Remick et al., *Investigating Complaints of Sexual Harassment, in* IVORY POWER: SEXUAL HARASSMENT ON CAMPUS (M. Paludi ed., 1990). C. SHATTUCK & K. WILLIAMS, EMPLOYER'S GUIDE TO CONTROLLING SEXUAL HARASSMENT (1992).
2. B. Gutek & M. Koss, *Changed Women and Changed Organizations: Consequences of and Coping with Sexual Harassment,* JOURNAL OF VOCATIONAL BEHAVIOR 42, at 28–48.
3. K. Quina, *The Victimization of Women, in* IVORY POWER: SEXUAL HARASSMENT ON CAMPUS (M. Paludi ed., 1990).

The Role
of the EEOC
in Sexual
Harassment
Situations

. . . the primary responsibility of this committee is fairness. That means making sure that we do not victimize any witness who appears here and that we treat every witness with respect. And without making any judgment about the specific witnesses we will hear from today, fairness means understanding what a victim of sexual harassment goes through, why victims often do not report such crimes, why they often believe that they should or cannot leave their jobs. . . . Fairness means doing our best to understand, no matter what we do or do not believe about the specific charges.

—Senator Biden,
Senate Judiciary Confirmation Hearings
of Clarence Thomas, 1991

CASE STUDY

Jennifer Jones has been working in an environment that has intermittently been very uncomfortable for her. When she first came into the shop, she was constantly the focus of sexual innuendos and comments and belittling statements about her ability to do the job. For the past seven months, however, the shop has been rather quiet until one morning when the supervisor brings in a new pinup calendar from one of the suppliers. The men call her over and show her the calendar, asking why she isn't on it. They continue ridiculing her because she didn't "make it" into the pictures until the supervisor grows tired of the joke and tells everyone to get back to work.

Jennifer is crushed because she thought the problem was over. She knows that her company has a sexual harassment policy and procedure, but it requires that she report the problem to her supervisor first. Finally, after talking to a friend on the phone, she takes a long lunch and walks over to the EEOC office, where she files an official complaint. When her supervisor hears about her complaint, he is furious and wants to fire her for not using internal procedures. Can Jennifer do this? What is the best way for the company to handle the situation? Can it ask the EEOC to back off because the company has its own policy?

Introduction

As has been previously stated, the Equal Employment Opportunity Commission is the federal agency that is granted the authority to carry out the requirements of Title VII. A basic understanding of how the EEOC operates and the process for dealing with complaints is important in a complete picture of the law and sexual harassment. In this chapter, we will discuss the EEOC's procedures, but many employees will be involved with local rather than federal agencies. Whereas many follow much the same procedures of complaint filing and conciliation, it is important to check with any applicable local agencies. A list showing examples of such agencies is included in the appendix. Usually, they will have booklets available that will describe the agencies' procedures and help in understanding what to expect.

The Authority of the EEOC

The EEOC was created by the Civil Rights Act of 1964, in which the EEOC was granted the authority to investigate and conciliate complaints that alleged a violation of the law of employment discrimination. In 1972, Title VII was amended to also grant the EEOC the power to bring court actions in certain cases on behalf of victims of discrimination.

The EEOC has been instrumental in a variety of ways in shaping the law of sexual harassment. It has issued guidelines and policy statements to help employers understand the ever-changing law in this area. For example, its *Guidelines for Discrimination on the Basis of Sex*[1] provides the basic definition that is usually quoted in regard to sexual harassment. In addition, the EEOC has brought a number of lawsuits that were pivotal in developing the law and has filed *amicus* briefs[2] in many lawsuits and appeals brought by private individuals. The EEOC was quoted several times by the United States Supreme Court in its decisions in *Meritor Savings Bank v. Vinson* and *Harris v. Forklift Systems,* the sexual harassment cases discussed in chapter 2.

The EEOC has authority under Title VII to pursue complaints for parties who feel that they have had their equal employment rights violated. Although Title VII does not prohibit lawsuits by private parties, it requires that employees first file a charge of discrimination with the EEOC before they are allowed to go to court for themselves. Charges may be filed with the EEOC in person, by mail, or by telephone. In states or localities where there is an antidiscrimination law and an agency authorized to grant or seek relief, a charge must be presented to that state or local agency.

Statutes of Limitations

There are strict statutes of limitations, or time periods, in which complaints must be filed. Title VII specifies that a charge must be filed within 180 days of the alleged discriminatory act. In situations where a claim is required to be brought to the state or local agency first, the EEOC complaint may be filed within three hundred days of the discriminatory act or thirty days after receiving notice that the state or local agency has terminated its processing of the charge, whichever is earlier. A party may also request that a charge be forwarded by the state agency to the EEOC.

In certain situations, courts will allow a charge for acts that occurred outside the time periods. This would occur when the EEOC and the courts decide that the situation involves what is called in the law a *continuing violation.* Often, a sexual harassment claim involves several acts of discrimination (such as the belittling comments in the case study), but only one of the acts is within the statutory limits. Under the continuing violation doctrine, despite the fact that only one act occurred in the time limit, all of the conduct can become part of the claim.

> *In the case study, the behavior that occurred seven months before her complaint may become part of Jennifer's case if the EEOC and/or a court feels that they are part of the same pattern of discrimination.*

An inappropriate response to a sexual harassment claim may be the one act within the time frame that brings in all the other discriminatory acts. Once again, it is vital that the employer's process or lack of process not itself be part of the problem.

The EEOC Investigation

The EEOC, after receiving the complaint, may begin an investigation to determine whether there is merit to the claim. First, the potential plaintiff will be interviewed to determine as much information as possible and to find out whether all of the legal jurisdictional requirements, such as the statutes of limitations, have been met. The charge will then be properly prepared, and the investigation procedure explained to the person making the complaint.

Next, the EEOC notifies the employer about the charge. The EEOC will usually request that a fact-finding conference be held at which an EEOC specialist will try to work out a settlement. Whereas the advice of the company's attorney is probably appropriate at this time, resistance or anger is usually not a useful or beneficial response. After all, a business that has exercised good business sense should have nothing to hide, and if there is a problem, this may be the last possible point at which to control liability costs. The courts are clear that, even if the employer had no notice before the charge is filed, there *is* notice once the EEOC informs the company. If the problem was not adequately handled before, it should be handled at this point to minimize a much greater potential expense later.

In this investigation, the EEOC may try to solve the problems informally using what Title VII calls methods of "conference, conciliation, and persuasion." If the evidence has shown that there is reasonable cause to believe that discrimination has occurred, the agency will attempt to persuade the employer to voluntarily eliminate or remedy the problem. It may seek, among other remedies, reinstatement of the employee, back pay, and/or restoration of lost benefits. A business that digs in its heels and refuses to acknowledge that it has not done what it should in this situation can only increase its liability and cost. If the situation wasn't handled correctly before, it should be done at the conciliation stage.

During these informal proceedings, Title VII provides protection for the employer who is working with the EEOC to try to resolve the situation. The law provides that "[n]othing said or done during and as a part of such informal endeavors may be made public by the Commission . . . or used as evidence in a subsequent proceeding." Thus, materials revealed to the EEOC or statements made during this time could not be admitted as evidence against the company should the case end up in court.

If conciliation fails, the EEOC considers the case for a lawsuit in the federal courts. This case would be filed by the agency on behalf of the complaining party or parties, and the EEOC would bear the cost of the litigation. This process could take many years, and the potential for appeals and the legal costs to the employer could be extensive.

Right to Sue

At any stage of the investigation, the EEOC may determine, for a variety of reasons, that it is not going to pursue the complaint. In addition, after ninety days has elapsed from the filing of the complaint, the complainant may ask the agency for the right to take the case to court.

In order for a private lawsuit to be filed under Title VII, the EEOC must issue what is called a "right to sue" letter to the employee who made the complaint. The employee then has ninety days in which to file a private lawsuit in federal or state court. Even though the EEOC chooses not to pursue the complaint, this does not necessarily mean that there is no merit to the claim. An employer should not automatically assume that the matter is then concluded. Many such claims are decided in favor of the complaining parties; the EEOC's refusal to pursue may be based merely on the agency's budgetary constraints.

Once a private party has filed a federal lawsuit under Title VII, the EEOC is usually no longer involved with the claim. In a few instances, it may intervene as an *amicus,* as discussed before, but usually it will have no further dealings with either party.

Lawsuits

Whereas the resolution of the claim in an agency proceeding is probably better for minimizing costs, the increasing number of complaints filed with the EEOC makes it likely today that the agency will not be involved and that the plaintiff will end up in court. At this point, if the employer has done all that can be expected, a request to the judge for a summary judgment may be in order. A summary judgment means that the judge has determined from the pleadings, the written declarations by the plaintiff and defendant, that a trial is unnecessary and one party is entitled by law to win.

Recent studies of current practice in sexual harassment cases show that a defendant is most likely to be granted a summary judgment only in cases where there is a legally defensible policy and appropriate responses. Rarely will a judge step in before trial for other possible defenses. For example, a claim that this behavior was welcomed or that it did not affect a term or condition of employment—that the behavior was not serious enough—is unlikely to result in a summary judgment. Judges are too aware of the expanding and amorphous nature of sexual harassment to make a decision before all of the facts, witnesses, and evidence have been presented. Most likely, under current law, this presentation will be before a jury, and as every lawyer can tell you, juries are usually involved when huge damages are awarded.

When an Employee Turns to the EEOC

After putting together and carrying out an extensive sexual harassment policy and program, any problems should have been dealt with internally and without government intervention. There is always the potential, however, even if a company adopts a strong policy and procedure, that an employee will not take advantage of the opportunity to internally handle the problem. She or he may choose, for whatever reason, to go directly to a government agency such as the EEOC and file a complaint. There is nothing to prevent this from happening, and a company need not become defensive if it does. A request from an agency for a fact-finding conference is not a challenge, and no determination has been made that the complaint is valid. It must be remembered that the EEOC is most interested, in the beginning, in finding out exactly what happened and conciliating or settling the matter amicably between the two parties.

If the employer has done what is expected, there is probably little to worry about if a complaint is filed. There is every possibility that the EEOC will find that there is no merit in the complaint, and that will be the end of the matter, as far as the agency is concerned. Of course, an employee has an option to file a lawsuit, but from all the cases being decided today, there is every indication that an employer would win a case when it can show that it has done all that was required: its policy and procedures are seriously carried out; it encourages reporting and handles complaints in an effective and efficient manner; harassed employees do not suffer adverse consequences; discipline is designed to prevent any reoccurrences; retaliation is not allowed; and training is provided and required on an ongoing basis. The company meant what it said in its policies and procedures and indicated this in no uncertain terms from the CEO on down. There is nothing more that the law can ask with regard to removing the opportunity for a hostile environment to exist—and, in fact, it does not.

However, there is always the possibility that something did go amiss with regard to the policy or that this is a *quid pro quo* situation, where even the most extensive internal program may not be a defense.

> *In the case study, it is evident that the company's policy did not contain a fail-safe provision, which led to Jennifer turning to the EEOC. Once the company hears about the complaint from the government agency, it should immediately figure out how to solve the problem to Jennifer's satisfaction. Then it should solve the problem with the policy so that other employees don't feel the need to go outside the internal procedures.*

Summary

It should be apparent that there are many stages at which complaints may be handled, and that as it progresses through these stages, a complaint becomes more and more expensive. Once again, the smartest course for a business is to "take care of business" at the earliest possible point. Adopt a process that handles any sexual harassment situation appropriately right at the start. If the process doesn't, handle the situation when the agency gives notice. If the situation goes beyond that point, the costs can be staggering, both economically and public relations-wise.

There are three possible scenarios, then, that are satisfactory for an employer dealing with sexual harassment. The first and best is that the EEOC or a state or local agency will never call because the business's employees are satisfied and happy with the internal program and procedures, which are handling complaints before the point of legal liability is ever approached. The second best is that the EEOC gives notice of a complaint, and the employer responds calmly and confidently because it has done everything that is necessary to minimize liability, and it knows the process has worked correctly. The third is that an agency gives notice and the employer, after responding calmly and confidently, determines that a problem has occurred, despite its best efforts, and remedies the problem immediately. Any other scenario evidences an attitude that is foolish, time consuming, and costly, and that reflects bad business judgment.

> *Take a final look at the case study. The supervisor wants to fire Jennifer for going to the EEOC, an angry reaction to what he may view as insubordinate behavior. Doing so, however, could be viewed as retaliation for Jennifer's exercising rights granted to employees under Title VII, a clear violation of the law. By firing Jennifer, the supervisor not only may get the company into some possibly heavy damages but may allow all of the previous months' behavior to become part of the case on the continuing violation doctrine. Such a response makes no business sense.*

For Reflection

1. Discuss why the company's response to the EEOC is so important.

2. Discuss why you think the law sets up statutes of limitations. What is gained by them? What is lost? What do you think about the 180 days requirement?

3. Why do you think that the courts began using the continuing violation doctrine? Do you agree that it is a good idea? Why or why not?

4. Why do you think the "right to sue" letter is required by the law? Why can plaintiffs not go directly to court? What role did the law expect for the EEOC?

5. Some employers believe that a complaint from the EEOC means that a lawsuit is imminent. Discuss why that is not necessarily true.

6. Why do you think that the law restricts the use of information gained during an EEOC investigation? Do you think that this is a good policy? Why or why not?

Notes

1. 29 CFR Sec 1601.
2. An *amicus curiae* brief is a written presentation of a point of view that is filed with a court when the party is not a plaintiff or a defendant in the case. The court must approve a request to file an *amicus* brief and usually does so when it feels that the individual or organization making the request has some relevant information or an important perspective to add to the issue(s) being decided.

Appendices

APPENDIX

Resources for Conducting Training Programs on Sexual Harassment

The organization's policy statement and grievance procedures must be communicated to all employees. Employees must know their rights and responsibilities with respect to being a complainant, an accused, and a witness. The most effective way to communicate the grievance procedure and policy statement is through training programs. There are several steps to designing and implementing a training program on sexual harassment. We identify and discuss each of these steps in this appendix.

Issues to Consider before Training

Conduct a needs assessment. There are several topics to be discussed in any training program on sexual harassment (e.g., legal definition, Sexual Harassment Trauma Syndrome, the organization's policy and grievance procedures). We also recommend conducting a needs assessment (see exhibit 1) with the administrative staff of an organization in order to identify additional issues

EXHIBIT 1

Needs Assessment

INTRODUCTION

We are seeking assistance with advancing the understanding of sexual harassment. As part of our effort, you are being asked to complete the following brief survey based on your needs for and expectations of future training sessions on issues related to sexual harassment.

Your participation in this survey will help me in my role as a consultant to more fully understand the organizational climate and culture in your company and best represent your needs.

This is an anonymous survey. All replies will be kept confidential. Any information used from this survey will be used in aggregate form with no reference to individual responses.

I appreciate the time you are taking to complete and return this important survey.

PART 1: DEMOGRAPHIC INFORMATION

1. What is your age?
   (Please check appropriate category)

20–25____	46–50____
26–30____	51–55____
31–35____	56–60____
36–40____	61–65____
41–45____	65+____

2. What is your racial/ethnic background?
   (Please check the appropriate category)
   African American   ____
   Asian American   ____
   Euro-American   ____
   Hispanic/Latino   ____
   Native American   ____
   Multiracial   ____
   Other____ (please specify) _____

3. What is your sex?
   Female____
   Male   ____

4. Are you physically challenged?

Yes____

No____

Please specify:_____

PART 2: NEEDS ASSOCIATED WITH TRAINING IN SEXUAL HARASSMENT

1. Some of the goals of training in issues related to sexual harassment are

   defining sexual harassment

   providing incidence rates

   providing a profile of a sexual harassment victim

   providing a profile of harassers

   how to file a complaint of sexual harassment

   Which of these goals do you consider most important? Why? Are there other goals you would add to this list? If so, please identify them and indicate why you believe they are important. Use the space below to write your answer. Should you need more space, please use the reverse side of this sheet.

2. Which of the following activities would be most important to the future of dealing with sexual harassment in your company?

   educating managers

   educating employees

   revising the policy

   having a new investigator

3. In your opinion, what indications are there that individuals in your company are not trained in issues related to sexual harassment?

4. In your opinion, how can the need for training individuals be met most effectively?

5. In your opinion, what is the state of readiness for a training program on sexual harassment?

6. Please complete the following sentences:

   Things I would like to understand better about sexual harassment are . . .

   Things I would like to learn how to do better with respect to dealing with sexual harassment in my company are . . .

   Feelings I have in my company regarding sexual harassment that I would like to change or improve are . . .

7. Indicate below (using check marks) whether you would like the information to be included in a training session on sexual harassment:

Topic	Yes—Include in Training	No—Don't Include in Training
sexual orientation	_____	_____
ethnicity and race	_____	_____
racism	_____	_____
homophobia	_____	_____
abuses of power	_____	_____
verbal communication styles	_____	_____
nonverbal communication styles	_____	_____
empowerment of diverse populations	_____	_____
reporting techniques	_____	_____
profiles of harassers	_____	_____
impact of sexual harassment on victims	_____	_____

Additional comments you wish to make:

I welcome your comments about any of the items in the survey and additional information about the training programs being developed for your company that you would like to share with me. Thank you again.

they expect to be covered in a training session. Examples of these additional topics include (1) the interface of racial harassment and sexual harassment, (2) the role the Employees Assistance Program plays in counseling individuals involved in a sexual harassment complaint procedure, and (3) the interface of homophobia and sexual harassment. The topics are typically suggested to a trainer based on the organization's prior complaints.

The following needs assessment is proposed for determining training programs on sexual harassment.

1. Identify groups and individuals to be involved in needs assessment (e.g., managerial staff).

2. Ask individuals to provide answers to questions regarding sexual harassment in the workplace via an anonymous mail survey.

3. Facilitate two-hour focus groups or roundtable discussions with randomly selected employees (twenty per session) to elicit in-depth responses (see exhibit 2). Structured interview questions for individuals who participate in the focus groups center around employees' goals for training sessions, including their

Sample Interview Questions
for Roundtable Discussions with Managers

(Total Time Required Per Focus Group: 2 Hours)

PART 1: INTRODUCTION AND OVERVIEW
OF FOCUS GROUP

(10–15 minutes)

VERBAL OVERVIEW

As you know, this company is seeking assistance with advancing the understanding and management of sexual harassment. A few weeks ago, you were asked to complete a brief anonymous survey regarding the issues you would like to see addressed in training sessions on sexual harassment.

Today, you are being asked to participate in a focus group/ roundtable discussion to help me in my role as a consultant to more fully understand the organizational climate and culture in your company and best represent your needs (in aggregate form, not to be singled out in any way) for planning training sessions.

INTRODUCTION OF TRAINER.

INTRODUCTIONS OF INDIVIDUALS
PARTICIPATING IN FOCUS GROUPS.

PART 2: FOCUS GROUP STRUCTURED QUESTIONS

(10–15 minutes per question; participants offer viewpoints.)
(Responses will be written on flip chart for all participants to see.)

> What specifically do you want to accomplish in your company in the next two years?
>
> How will training programs on sexual harassment in the workplace help facilitate you achieving these goals?
>
> What specifically do you want to cover in training sessions in order to help you achieve your goals?
>
> Identify two things you need to help you feel more empowered as a manager in your company.

Identify two things you hope the training programs will help you to identify and manage.

What do you believe is the state of readiness for a training program on sexual harassment in your company?

PART 3: SUMMARY

Trainer reviews comments generated from managers in focus groups. Trainer asks for additional comments related to future training sessions.

Trainer allows time for individuals to discuss their concerns with her or him individually.

needs with regard to better understanding victims of sexual harassment and individuals with viewpoints and mind-sets different from their own.

4. Analyze responses from steps 2 and 3 using qualitative and quantitative statistical analyses.
5. Prepare a written report that summarizes the needs assessment, including suggestions for the following:

   How to increase awareness

   Ways to examine attitudes

   Alternatives to stereotyping

   Methods of supportive action
6. Make recommendations for post-training evaluations.

Thus the major goal of the proposed needs assessment is to obtain information concerning the manner in which sexual harassment is addressed in the organizational climate of the company, including topics such as empowerment, establishment of mutual trust and respect, methods of inclusion or exclusion, verbal and nonverbal communication, empowering employees in the process. Thus the process of the assessment will be consistent with the goal of the training programs in which the employees will subsequently participate.

Identify the goals and objectives of the training session. The goals for sexual harassment training for most organizations are

1. to provide all members of the organization with a clear understanding of their rights and responsibilities;
2. to enable individuals to distinguish between behavior that is sexual harassment and is not sexual harassment;
3. to provide individuals with information concerning the policy statement against sexual harassment and grievance procedures set up by the organization;

4. to set up an environment that is free of sexual harassment and free of the fear of being retaliated against for speaking about sexual harassment.

Once the goals have been established, the following steps *must* be taken prior to the beginning of the training sessions:

1. Develop or revise the organization's policy statement against sexual harassment. Because the policy statement is part of the training session content, it must be completed prior to training.
2. Develop or revise grievance procedures for handling complaints of sexual harassment. Grievance procedures are part of the content of the training and thus should be developed prior to training.

The CEO should invite all employees to participate in a training session. The most important feature of effective grievance procedures to investigate complaints of sexual harassment for any organization is the training programs designed to implement this policy. Effective training programs send a clear message to all employees that the sexual harassment procedures must be taken seriously and that sexual harassment will not be tolerated by management. If the organization wants to demonstrate its determination to stop sexual harassment, the CEO must actively participate in the training session and not give the verbal or nonverbal message that she or he is simply going through the motions. The CEO must set a tone that suggests that the organization will not tolerate sexual harassment, and that training is needed for all members of the organization, including those individuals who hold most of the organizational power.

All employees must be informed about their rights and responsibilities with respect to sexual harassment. Their participation in a training session should be mandatory. Optional attendance at a training session conveys management's belief that it is not worth devoting three or four hours to the topic of sexual harassment. The commitment to addressing sexual harassment must be put in writing to all members of the organization by the CEO. This administrator must also demand all employees' participation at training sessions. The letter or memo must be written in a straightforward and nonthreatening manner. Flexibility in accommodating work schedules must be maintained. We suggest the CEO maintain a record of all employees who fail to participate in a training session. A letter to this effect should be placed in an employee's personnel file.

Design training sessions for groups of individuals working together in a department or organization. Training sessions can be established for individuals within certain departments because they each have unique responsibilities. Training sessions for investigators of complaints of sexual harassment should be separate from other training programs. In exhibit 3, we present a sample outline for training investigators of complaints.

In addition, some organizations request training programs for their employees who have been selected to provide the training programs for the

---

EXHIBIT 3

Sample Outline of Training Program for Investigators

The goals of the training program are to

provide information concerning liability,

define *quid pro quo* and hostile environment sexual harassment,

discuss psychological issues involved in dealing with sexual harassment,

discuss the physical and emotional reactions to being sexually harassed,

discuss means of resolution for complaints of sexual harassment.

At the conclusion of this training program, investigators will be able to

assess their own perceptions of the definition, incidence, and psychological dimensions of sexual harassment;

adequately label behaviors as illustrative of sexual harassment or not illustrative of sexual harassment;

assess why individuals choose to report or not report sexual harassment;

identify peer sexual harassment;

identify employees' rights and responsibilities under Title VII;

design educational programs to deal with sexual harassment, including peer sexual harassment;

adequately interview complainants and individuals about whom complaints have been filed.

TOPICS FOR PRESENTATION AND DISCUSSION

Part 1   Introduction to training session and goals of seminar/workshop

Part 2   The complainant's perspective

Part 3   Psychology of the victimization process
Internally and externally focused strategies
Psychology of reporting incidents of sexual harassment

Part 4   The accused's perspective

Part 5   Differential evaluations of identical behavior

Part 6   Keeping investigative process consistent with responses to sexual harassment by individuals involved

Break
Part 7   Interviewing techniques
Part 8   Note taking and record keeping
Part 9   Case studies
Part 10 Summary and general discussion
Break
Part 11 Role-play exercises

entire company. These programs are referred to as "train-the-trainer" seminars. A sample outline of the issues to be presented in a train-the-trainer seminar is presented in exhibit 4.

EXHIBIT 4

Sample Outline of Training Program for "Train the Trainers"

CONTENT TRAINING

The goals of the training program are to

provide information concerning liability,

define *quid pro quo* and hostile environment sexual harassment,

discuss psychological issues involved in dealing with sexual harassment,

discuss the physical and emotional reactions to being sexually harassed,

provide a psychological profile of sexual harassers,

discuss peer sexual harassment,

discuss means of resolution for complaints of sexual harassment.

At the conclusion of this training program, trainers will be able to

assess their own perceptions of the definition, incidence, and psychological dimensions of sexual harassment;

adequately label behaviors as illustrative of sexual harassment or not illustrative of sexual harassment;

assess why individuals choose to report or not report sexual harassment;

identify peer sexual harassment;
identify employees' rights and responsibilities under Title VII.

TOPICS FOR PRESENTATION AND DISCUSSION

PART 1   INTRODUCTION TO TRAINING SESSION AND GOALS OF SEMINAR/WORKSHOP

(20 minutes)

Trainer welcomes participants to seminar.
Trainer introduces herself or himself to participants and indicates responsibility in establishing a climate free of sexual harassment.
Participants introduce themselves and state their goals for the training session.
Trainer writes these goals on the flip chart or chalkboard for all participants to see.
Trainer summarizes goals.
Trainer lectures on the major components of the training session.

PART 2   PERCEPTIONS VERSUS REALITIES IN SEXUAL HARASSMENT

(20 minutes)

Trainer summarizes individuals' responses to questions concerning sexual harassment.
Trainer makes summary comments from this unit.

PART 3   DEFINITION OF SEXUAL HARASSMENT

(30 minutes)

Trainer lectures and leads guided discussion of sexual harassment:
 summary of case law on *quid pro quo* and hostile environment sexual harassment
 behavioral examples of sexual harassment
 peer sexual harassment
Trainer makes summary comments from this unit.

PART 4 INCIDENCE OF SEXUAL HARASSMENT

(20 minutes)

Trainer lectures on the incidence of workplace sexual harassment:
measurement considerations
underreporting of incidences
individuals at risk for sexual harassment
relationship between incidence and reporting
Trainer makes summary comments from this unit.

BREAK—10 MINUTES

PART 5 IMPACT OF SEXUAL HARASSMENT
ON INDIVIDUALS AND WORKPLACE

(25 minutes)

Trainer lectures on the impact of sexual harassment on employees.
Trainer lectures on the cost of sexual harassment for the workplace.
Trainer makes summary comments from this unit.

PART 6 CAUSES OF SEXUAL HARASSMENT

(20 minutes)

Trainer lectures on explanatory models of sexual harassment.
Trainer lectures on psychological profiles of harassers.
Trainer makes summary comments from this unit.

PART 7 PREVENTING SEXUAL HARASSMENT
IN THE WORKPLACE

(45 minutes)

Trainer lectures on the components of an effective policy statement for employees.
Trainer discusses grievance procedures.
Trainer makes summary comments from this unit.

PART 8   SUMMARY COMMENTS AND REVIEW

(30 minutes)

Trainer lectures on myths and realities of sexual harassment.
Trainer leads general discussion of sexual harassment.
Trainer asks participants to reread case study and answer questions.
Trainer reviews participants' goals that were generated at the beginning of the session.
Question and answer period.

LUNCH BREAK—1½ HOURS

PEDAGOGY TRAINING

The goals of the training program are to

provide information concerning creating an atmosphere conducive to training employees;
discuss use of role-playing, case studies, and scenarios in training employees;
discuss use of pre-training and post-training surveys.

At the conclusion of this training program, trainers will be able to

assess their own perceptions of their ability to provide training for employees,
adequately address questions concerning content,
administer surveys to assess attitudes and prevalence regarding sexual harassment.

TOPICS FOR PRESENTATION AND DISCUSSION

PART 1   INTRODUCTION TO PEDAGOGY TRAINING

(20 minutes)

Discuss attitudes of employees in attending training sessions on sexual harassment.
Discuss ways to empower employees who are participating in sexual harassment training.
Trainer summarizes goals.

**PART 2   NOTIFYING EMPLOYEES THAT THEY WILL
PARTICIPATE IN TRAINING SESSIONS**

(20 minutes)

**PART 3   PRESENTING MATERIAL ON SEXUAL
HARASSMENT TO EMPLOYEES**

(60 minutes)

Definitions of sexual harassment
Impact of sexual harassment on individuals and workplace
Effective verbal and nonverbal communication strategies
Explanatory models of sexual harassment

BREAK—10 MINUTES

**PART 4   DEALING WITH ANGER, FRUSTRATION,
AND ANXIETY ON THE PART OF
EMPLOYEES PARTICIPATING
IN TRAINING SESSIONS**

(60 minutes)

**PART 5   HOW TO DISCUSS POLICY STATEMENT
AND GRIEVANCE PROCEDURES
IN TRAINING SESSION**

(30 minutes)

PART 6   SUMMARY COMMENTS AND REVIEW

(30 minutes)

Develop resources for participants in training sessions. Training sessions are an area for disseminating information about the organization's policy against sexual harassment, as well as for discussing sexual harassment in
general. Pamphlets or handouts describing the following information must be
distributed to all participants in the training session:

legal definition of sexual harassment
behavioral definitions of sexual harassment

grievance procedures at the organization
name and phone numbers/office numbers of investigators
locations where information may be obtained on sexual harassment
information regarding stress effects of sexual harassment
policy statement against sexual harassment

Assess the participants' concerns about sexual harassment prior to the training session. Frequently, participants in training sessions question the high incidence reported with respect to victims of sexual harassment in the workplace. They also commonly state that "It's not that bad here where we work." Such comments made in the training session inhibit individuals from speaking about their own concerns and subsequently filing a complaint. In order to address the incidence and dimensions of sexual harassment at the particular company, it is helpful to disseminate an anonymous questionnaire that asks employees about sexual harassment. Results from this questionnaire can be used as part of the training session. The trainer should develop and analyze responses from these surveys.

Issues to Consider during Training

SPECIFIC OBJECTIVES

The specific goals of sexual harassment training programs are to

1. educate employees about the legal definitions and behavioral examples of *quid pro quo* and hostile environment sexual harassment;
2. discuss the physical and emotional reactions to being sexually harassed;
3. provide employees with a clear understanding of their rights and responsibilities;
4. encourage employees to examine their personal feelings and those of others;
5. dispel myths about sexual harassers;
6. explore responsible behavior in dealing with sexual harassers;
7. examine the effects of sexual harassment on employees, their families, and co-workers;
8. empower employees to take control of their behavior;
9. discuss female and male verbal and nonverbal communication styles;
10. discuss the company's central role in preventing sexual harassment.

Training sessions must be at least three hours in length and provided for the entire organization within a short time period. Sexual harassment training involves much more than a recitation of individuals' rights and responsibilities and what the law and company policy require. Training also requires dealing with individuals' assumptions and misconceptions about sexual harassment and their anxieties about the training itself. Thus, training sessions must devote ample time to dealing with the participants' feelings, misconceptions, and questions. All sessions must be completed within a few weeks. It is best to schedule a maximum of thirty to thirty-five individuals per training session so as to have ample discussion and contribution from all participants.

Training sessions must build in time for questions from individuals who wish to speak privately to the trainer. Frequently, individuals in training sessions want to discuss their concerns with the trainer alone, without hearing any comments from other participants. Because sexual harassment involves sexuality, it is not like other forms of discrimination. Individuals often view sexual harassment as intimate and sexual and therefore difficult to discuss in public.

Training programs should include both women and men as participants. One of the consistent research findings in sexual harassment concerns the differential perceptions of the same event by women and men. Women tend to view sexual harassment as an abuse of power; men tend to view sexual harassment as flirtation and flattery. In training sessions, many women are pleased that the issue finally will be addressed; many men are worried that they can't joke or have fun with women anymore. It is helpful to have women and men included in the same training sessions so that these differential perceptions can be identified and discussed. Separate sessions for women and men may perpetuate stereotypes that all men are guilty of sexual harassment and all women are victims. This latter type of training is also divisive and contributes to further harassment of women by men. Both women and men have the same rights and responsibilities with respect to sexual harassment and must be provided the same information concerning these rights and responsibilities.

Additional issues. The following considerations must be well thought out before the initiation of any training program:

1. What provisions does the company have for employees who wish to report an experience that was prompted from the training?
2. Does the company have trained therapists available during and following the training session to assist any employee who has a "flashback" or is visibly upset after the training?
3. What means of reinforcing the information from the training program has the company instituted?

Issues to Consider after Training

Conduct follow-up surveys. It is recommended that three and six month follow-up surveys be disseminated to all employees in order to determine

1. whether they have noticed a difference in the climate since the training sessions,
2. whether they feel the training sessions helped them feel better about the organization,

3. whether they believe the training sessions made it possible to discuss sexual harassment without the fear of retaliation,
4. whether they believe the company continues to take the issue of sexual harassment seriously.

Hold training sessions annually. It is recommended that the organization hold training sessions on sexual harassment annually at new employee orientations. Materials on sexual harassment must also be included in employee handbooks. A statement from the CEO outlining the organization's policy against sexual harassment must be reissued annually.

Educational Qualifications of Trainers

There are several recommended characteristics of good trainers of sexual harassment programs. We can recommend the following educational qualifications that should be evaluated by any company seeking training in sexual harassment:

1. Knowledge of psychological theories of sexual harassment and of power is helpful when training employees. Trainers must be able to explain psychological terms in nontechnical terms for employees.
2. Knowledge of the psychology of work and careers.
3. Knowledge of research and theories on gender-role socialization. This knowledge must include socialization agents (i.e., parents, peers, media, teachers, music), theories of gender role acquisition, and research on verbal and nonverbal communication skills;
4. Knowledge of recent case law and legislation is mandatory for trainers.
5. Fluency in languages in addition to English (or have a cotrainer who can meet this need).

We recommend that trainers be interviewed in person by a few individuals who represent the group of individuals for whom the training will be provided. Areas of inquiry include

1. education or training in the psychological issues involved in sexual harassment;
2. education or training in the legal issues involved in this area;
3. publications or presentations on the topic;
4. list of previous training seminars or workshops and individuals who can give recommendations about previous training programs;
5. outlines or videotapes of previous training seminars or workshops;
6. familiarity with companies of the size of the present one;
7. ability to work with administrators, including human resource specialists;
8. education or training in psychological issues involved in facilitating a training program.

Personality Characteristics of Trainers

One of the repeated findings from research and education and training programs at companies concerns the resistance to talking about sexual harassment. These experiences are difficult to discuss, the topic taps the experiences of many individuals, resolutions may seem out of reach and burdensome, and the behaviors are occurring to someone we know or ourselves at the time we are participating in a training program. Although we may want to avoid discussing sexual harassment, we have little choice: sexual harassment is reaching epidemic proportions and it must be addressed.

Questions that dominate the training sessions tend to be classified into two major types: those that deal with the nature of sexual harassment and abuse, and those that reflect a frustration about the topic. Employees' questions reflect fear and confusion surrounding sexual harassment. The topic of sexual harassment arouses discomfort and defensiveness. Employees may want to joke about abuse. Would they joke that way in a training program on racial relations or AIDS? Most likely not. Training sessions on sexual harassment inevitably challenge widely held assumptions about female-male relationships and power that are not easy to change. Some employees may joke during the training session as a coping strategy.

It is important to give legitimacy to the anxieties, confusion, and fears raised by participants in the training programs. In addition, it is necessary to establish rapport and a respectful atmosphere in the training session. It is also important to talk up front about the attitudes individuals brought with them to the session, perhaps using the issues raised in national media accounts of an example of sexual harassment as a starting point.

It is imperative that trainers know that some employees may be experiencing sexual harassment, and that the anger they feel toward the perpetrator may be expressed to the trainer. Therapeutic support staff (e.g., EAP personnel) must be present during training programs to assist in this regard.

Sample Outline of Training Programs

In exhibit 5 we present a sample outline of a training program on sexual harassment for employees.

Note that we include in this outline the following topics we have discussed in detail throughout this book:

legal definition of sexual harassment
behavioral examples of sexual harassment
impact of sexual harassment on individuals and the organization
theoretical models to explain the occurrence of sexual harassment
the organization's commitment to preventing sexual harassment.

EXHIBIT 5

Sample Outline of Training Programs on Sexual Harassment For Employees

The Goals of the training program are to

provide information concerning liability,

define *quid pro quo* and hostile environment sexual harassment,

discuss psychological issues involved in dealing with sexual harassment,

discuss the physical and emotional reactions to being sexually harassed,

provide a psychological profile of sexual harassers,

discuss peer sexual harassment,

discuss means of resolution for complaints of sexual harassment.

At the conclusion of this training program, individuals will be able to

Assess their own perceptions of the definition, incidence, and psychological dimensions of sexual harassment;

Adequately label behaviors as illustrative of sexual harassment or not illustrative of sexual harassment;

Assess why individuals choose to report or not report sexual harassment;

Identify peer sexual harassment;

Identify employees' rights and responsibilities under Title VII.

TOPICS FOR PRESENTATION AND DISCUSSION

PART 1   INTRODUCTION TO TRAINING SESSION AND GOALS OF SEMINAR

Trainer welcomes participants to seminar.

Trainer introduces herself or himself, qualifications, background, etc.

Trainer summarizes goals of seminar.

Trainer asks each employee to state goal he or she has for the program.

Trainer writes each response on flip chart or chalkboard for all participants to see.

Trainer summarizes the goals of the participants in the training program.

PART 2   DEFINITION OF SEXUAL HARASSMENT

Summary of case law on *quid pro quo* and hostile environment sexual harassment.
Behavioral examples of sexual harassment.
Peer sexual harassment.
Trainer makes summary comments from this unit.

PART 3   IMPACT OF SEXUAL HARASSMENT ON INDIVIDUALS AND WORKPLACE ENVIRONMENT

Trainer discusses the impact of sexual harassment on employees.
Trainer discusses the cost of sexual harassment for the workplace.
Trainer makes summary comments from this unit.

PART 4   CAUSES OF SEXUAL HARASSMENT

Trainer highlights explanatory models of sexual harassment.
Trainer discusses psychological profiles of harassers.
Trainer makes summary comments from this unit.

PART 5   PREVENTING SEXUAL HARASSMENT

Importance of policy statement, grievance procedures, and training.
Trainer makes summary comments from this unit.
Trainer distributes copies of policy statement and grievance procedures.
Trainer introduces individual who is responsible for investigating complaints.

PART 6   SUMMARY COMMENTS AND REVIEW

Trainer summarizes major points from training program.
Trainer leads general discussion of sexual harassment.
General question and answer period.
Individual meetings with interested employees.

In addition to this technical information, we also included some pedagogical techniques, for example, welcoming the employees to the training program, asking employees to state a goal they have for the training session, and spending time with employees individually following the training program. We believe these pedagogical techniques are more important than any information that can be imparted during the training session. The techniques help foster a sense of trust, of commitment to the prevention of sexual harassment, and of respecting individuals' dignity. The pedagogical techniques thus model for the employees appropriate behavior in the workplace.

We can recommend additional issues to consider when implementing training programs:

1. The trainer should not use notes or read from any written material. Instead, she or he must maintain eye contact with the participants.

2. It is best for companies to hire an outside consultant who meets the educational qualifications and has the personality characteristics we outlined in this chapter. Human resource specialists at most companies cannot afford the time and commitment it takes to conduct the kind of in-depth sessions we have recommended.

3. Trainers can use case studies (ones we have discussed in this book work well) to stimulate discussion and to assist employees in understanding their responsibilities and sexual harassment in general.

4. A post-training evaluation is helpful. The trainer should keep in mind that she or he may not get the highest marks from individuals in the training session who are angry that they had to take this program in the first place. Trainers must not get discouraged but understand the psychology of the process of participating in a training session. In exhibit 6 we present a sample post-training evaluation form. A summary of the comments should be presented to the CEO of the company at which the training was held.

EXHIBIT 6

Sample Post-Training Evaluation Form

Thank you for completing this post-training evaluation form. Your responses are anonymous and will be kept confidential. Your responses will be helpful to me in developing future programs.

Please use the following scale in answering the questions:

3: Agree   2: Don't know/undecided   1: Disagree

I. ABOUT THE TRAINER

1. (Trainer's name) is knowledgeable about the issues.   3   2   1
2. (Trainer's name) has an effective communication style.   3   2   1

3. (Trainer's name) respected the participants in the session.   3   2   1
4. (Trainer's name) answered questions in a respectful manner.   3   2   1
5. (Trainer's name) treated participants as colleagues.   3   2   1
6. (Trainer's name) raised my awareness about the issues.   3   2   1

II. ABOUT THE CONTENT

1. The training program was organized.   3   2   1
2. The resource material will be helpful to me.   3   2   1
3. I learned the legal definition of sexual harassment.   3   2   1
4. I learned some behavioral examples of sexual harassment.   3   2   1
5. I was given some examples on how to monitor my own behavior with respect to sexual harassment.   3   2   1
6. I learned about power issues involved in sexual harassment.   3   2   1

III. ABOUT THE PROGRAM IN GENERAL

1. The objectives of the program were clearly identified.   3   2   1
2. The utilization of handouts enhanced the training.   3   2   1
3. Audiovisual equipment needs to be used in the training.   3   2   1
4. The acoustics and physical aspects of the room were sufficient.   3   2   1
5. The training increased my awareness of the issues.   3   2   1

IV. ABOUT MYSELF

1. I believe there is a commitment here to work on respecting the dignity of all people.   3   2   1
2. I feel that I benefited from participating in this training program.   3   2   1
3. I believe we need more training on these issues.   3   2   1

V. OVERALL RATING OF TRAINING PROGRAM

Please circle one of the following:

Good   Fair   Poor

VI. ADDITIONAL COMMENTS YOU WISH TO MAKE

Thank You!

APPENDIX

Selected Excerpts from the EEOC Guidelines

Equal Employment Opportunity Commission's Guidelines on Discrimination because of Sex

SEC 1604.11 SEXUAL HARASSMENT

(a) Harassment on the basis of sex is a violation of section 703 of title VII.[1] Unwelcome sexual advances, requests for sexual favors, and other verbal or physical conduct of a sexual nature constitute sexual harassment when (1) submission to such conduct is made either explicitly or implicitly a term or condition of an individual's employment, (2) submission to or rejection of such conduct by an individual is used as the basis for employment decisions affecting such individual, or (3) such conduct has the purpose or effect of unreasonably interfering with an individual's work performance or creating an intimidating, hostile, or offensive working environment.

(b) In determining whether alleged conduct constitutes sexual harassment, the Commission will look at the record as a whole and at the totality of the circumstances, such as the nature of the sexual advances and the context in which the alleged incidents occurred. The determination of the legality of a particular action will be made from the facts, on a case by case basis.

(c) Applying general title VII principles, an employer, employment agency, joint apprenticeship committee or labor organization (hereinafter collectively referred to as "employer") is responsible for its acts and those of its agents and supervisory employees with respect to sexual harassment regardless of whether the specific acts complained of were authorized or even forbidden by the employer and regardless of whether the employer knew or should have known of their occurrence. The Commission will examine the circumstances of the particular employment relationship and the job functions performed by the individual in determining whether an individual acts in either a supervisory or agency capacity.

(d) With respect to conduct between fellow employees, an employer is responsible for acts of sexual harassment in the workplace where the employer (or its agents or supervisory employees) knows or should have known of the conduct, unless it can show that it took immediate and appropriate corrective action.

(e) An employer may also be responsible for the acts of non-employees, with respect to sexual harassment of employees in the workplace, where the employer (or its agents or supervisory employees) knows or should have known of the conduct and fails to take immediate and appropriate corrective action. In reviewing these cases the Commission will consider the extent of the employer's control and any other legal responsibility which the employer may have with respect to the conduct of such non-employees.

(f) Prevention is the best tool for the elimination of sexual harassment. An employer should take all steps necessary to prevent sexual harassment from occurring, such as affirmatively raising the subject, expressing strong disapproval, developing appropriate sanctions, informing employees of their right to raise and how to raise the issue of harassment under title VII, and developing methods to sensitize all concerned.

(g) Other related practices: Where employment opportunities or benefits are granted because of an individual's submission to the employer's sexual advances or requests for sexual favors, the employer may be held liable for unlawful sex discrimination against other persons who were qualified for but denied that employment opportunity or benefit.

Notes

1. The principles involved here continue to apply to race, color, religion or national origin.

Equal Employment Opportunity Commission's Procedural Guidelines

SEC 1601.6 SUBMISSION OF INFORMATION

(a) The Commission shall receive information concerning alleged violations of Title VII . . . from any person. Where the information discloses that a person is entitled to file a charge with the Commission, the appropriate office shall render assistance in the filing of a charge. Any person or organization may request the issuance of a Commissioner charge for an inquiry into individual or systematic discrimination. Such request, with any pertinent information, should be submitted to the nearest field office.

(b) A person who submits data or evidence to the Commission may retain or, on payment of lawfully prescribed costs, procure a copy of transcript thereof, except that a witness may for good cause be limited to inspection of the official transcript of his or her testimony.

SEC. 1601.7 CHARGES BY OR ON BEHALF OF PERSONS CLAIMING TO BE AGGRIEVED

(a) A charge that any person has engaged in or is engaging in an unlawful employment practice within the meaning of Title VII . . . may be made by or on behalf of any person claiming to be aggrieved. A charge on behalf of a person claiming to be aggrieved may be made by any person, agency, or organization. The written charge need not identify by name the person on whose behalf it is made. The person making the charge, however, must provide the Commission with the name, address, and telephone number of the person on whose behalf the charge is made. During the Commission investigation, Commission personnel shall verify the authorization of such charge by the person on whose behalf the charge is made. Any such person may request that the Commission shall keep his or her identity confidential. . . .

SEC 1601.8 WHERE TO MAKE A CHARGE

A charge may be made in person or by mail at the offices of the Commission in Washington, D.C., or any of its field offices or with any designated representative of the Commission. The addresses of the Commission's field offices appear in Sec. 1610.4.

SEC 1601.12 CONTENTS OF CHARGE; AMENDMENT OF CHARGE

(a) Each charge should contain the following: (1) The full name, address and telephone number of the person making the charge except as provided in 1601.7;

(2) The full name and address of the person against whom the charge is made, if known (hereinafter referred to as the respondent); (3) A clear and concise statement of the facts, including pertinent dates, constituting the alleged unlawful employment practices: See § 1601.15(b); (4) If known, the approximate number of employees of the respondent employer or the approximate number of members of the respondent labor organization, as the case may be; and (5) A statement disclosing whether proceedings involving the alleged unlawful employment practice have been commenced before a State or local agency charged with the enforcement of fair employment practice laws and, if so, the date of such commencement and the name of the agency.

SEC 1601.18 DISMISSAL: PROCEDURE AND AUTHORITY

(a) Where a charge on its face, or as amplified by the statements of the person claiming to be aggrieved discloses, or where after investigation the Commission determines, that the charge and every portion thereof if not timely filed, or otherwise fails to state a claim under Title VII . . . the Commission shall dismiss the charge. . . .

(b) Where the person claiming to be aggrieved fails to provide requested necessary information, fails or refuses to appear or to be available for interviews or conferences as necessary, fails or refuses to provide information requested by the Commission . . . or otherwise refuses to cooperate to the extent that the Commission is unable to resolve the charge, and after due notice, the charging party has had 30 days in which to respond, the Commission may dismiss the charge.

(c) Where the person claiming to be aggrieved cannot be located, the Commission may dismiss the charge. . . .

(d) Where a respondent has made a settlement offer . . . which is in writing and specific in its terms, the Commission may dismiss the charge if the person claiming to be aggrieved refuses to accept the offer: *Provided,* That the offer would afford full relief for the harm alleged by the person . . .

SEC 1601.19 NO CAUSE DETERMINATIONS: PROCEDURE AND AUTHORITY

(a) Where the Commission completes its investigation of a charge and finds that there is not reasonable cause to believe that an unlawful employment practice has occurred or is occurring as to all issues addressed in the determination, the Commission shall issue a letter of determination to all parties to the charge indicating the finding. The Commission's letter of determination shall be the final determination of the Commission. The letter of determination shall inform the person claiming to be aggrieved or the person on whose behalf a charge was filed of the right to sue in Federal district court within 90 days of receipt of the letter of determination. . . .

SEC. 1601.21 REASONABLE CAUSE DETERMINATION: PROCEDURE AND AUTHORITY

(a) After completing its investigation, where the Commission has not settled or dismissed a charge or made a no cause finding as to every allegation . . . the Commission shall issue a determination that reasonable cause exists to believe that an unlawful employment practice has occurred or is occurring . . .

SEC. 1601.22 CONFIDENTIALITY

Neither a charge, nor information obtained during the investigation of a charge of employment discrimination . . . nor information obtained from records required to be kept or reports required to be filed . . . shall be made matters of public information by the Commission prior to the institution of any proceeding . . . involving such charge or information. . . .

SEC. 1601.24 CONCILIATION: PROCEDURE AND AUTHORITY

(a) Where the Commission determines that there is reasonable cause to believe that an unlawful employment practice has occurred or is occurring, the Commission shall endeavor to eliminate such practice by informal methods of conference, conciliation and persuasion. In conciliating a case . . . the Commission shall attempt to achieve a just resolution of all violations found and to obtain agreement that the respondent will eliminate the unlawful employment practice and provide appropriate affirmative relief. . . .

(c) Proof of compliance with Title VII . . . in accordance with the terms of the agreement shall be obtained by the Commission before the case is closed. . . .

SEC. 1601.25 FAILURE OF CONCILIATION; NOTICE

Where the Commission is unable to obtain voluntary compliance . . . and it determines that further efforts to do so would be futile or nonproductive, it shall . . . so notify the respondent in writing.

SEC. 1601.27 CIVIL ACTIONS BY THE COMMISSION

The Commission may bring a civil action against any respondent named in a charge . . . after thirty (30) days from the date of the filing of a charge with the

Commission unless a conciliation agreement acceptable to the Commission has been secured . . .

SEC. 1601.28 NOTICE OF RIGHT TO SUE: PROCEDURE AND AUTHORITY

(a) **Issuance of notice of right to sue upon request.** (1) When a person claiming to be aggrieved requests, in writing, that a notice of right to sue be issued . . . the Commission shall promptly issue such notice . . . to all parties, at any time after the expiration of one hundred eighty (180) days from the date of filing of the charge with the Commission . . .

(3) Issuance of a notice of right to sue shall terminate further proceeding of any charge . . .

(4) The issuance of a notice of right to sue does not preclude the Commission from offering such assistance to a person issued such notice as the Commission deems necessary or appropriate.

(b) **Issuance of notice of right to sue following Commission disposition of charge.** (1) Where the Commission has found reasonable cause to believe that Title VII . . . has been violated, has been unable to obtain voluntary compliance . . . and where the Commission has decided not to bring a civil action against the respondent, it will issue a notice of right to sue . . .

SEC. 1601.74 DESIGNATED AND NOTICE AGENCIES

(a) The designated FEP agencies are:

Alaska Commission for Human Rights
Alexandria (Va.) Human Rights Office
Allentown (Pa.) Human Relations Commission
Anchorage (Alaska) Equal Rights Commission
Anderson (Ind.) Human Relations Commission
Arizona Civil Rights Division
Arlington County (Va.) Human Rights Commission
Austin (Tex.) Human Relations Commission
Baltimore (Md.) Community Relations Commission
Bloomington (Ill.) Human Relations Commission
Bloomington (Ind.) Human Relations Commission
California Department of Fair Employment and Housing
Charleston (W.Va.) Human Rights Commission
City of Salina (Kans.) Human Relations Commission and Department
Clearwater (Fla.) Office of Community Relations
Colorado Civil Rights Commission

Colorado State Personnel Board
Commonwealth of Puerto Rico Department of Labor
Connecticut Commission on Human Rights and Opportunity
Corpus Christi (Tex.) Human Relations Commission
Dade County (Fla.) Fair Housing and Employment Commission
Delaware Department of Labor
District of Columbia Office of Human Rights
Durham (N.C.) Human Relations Commission
East Chicago (Ind.) Human Rights Commission
Evansville (Ind.) Human Relations Commission
Fairfax County (Va.) Human Rights Commission
Florida Commission on Human Relations
Fort Dodge–Webster County (Iowa) Human Rights Commission
Fort Wayne (Ind.) Metropolitan Human Relations Commission
Fort Worth (Tex.) Human Relations Commission
Gary (Ind.) Human Relations Commission
Georgia Office of Fair Employment Practices
Hawaii Department of Labor and Industrial Relations
Hillsborough County, Florida, Equal Opportunity and Human Relations Department
Howard County (Md.) Human Rights Commission
Huntington (W.Va.) Human Relations Commission
Idaho Human Rights Commission
Illinois Department of Human Rights
Indiana Civil Rights Commission
Iowa Civil Rights Commission
Jacksonville (Fla.) Equal Employment Opportunity Commission
Kansas City (Kans.) Human Relations Department
Kansas City (Mo.) Human Relations Department
Kansas Human Rights Commission
Kentucky Commission on Human Rights
Lee County (Fla.) Department of Equal Opportunity
Lexington-Fayette (Ky.) Urban County Human Rights Commission
Lincoln (Nebr.) Commission on Human Rights
Louisiana Commission on Human Rights
Louisville and Jefferson County (Ky.) Human Relations Commission
Madison (Wis.) Equal Opportunities Commission
Maine Human Rights Commission
Maryland Commission on Human Relations
Mason City, Iowa, Human Rights Commission
Massachusetts Commission Against Discrimination

Michigan City (Ind.) Human Rights Commission
Michigan Department of Civil Rights
Minneapolis (Minn.) Department of Civil Rights
Minnesota Department of Human Rights
Missouri Commission on Human Rights
Montana Human Rights Division
Montgomery County (Md.) Human Relations Commission
Nebraska Equal Opportunity Commission
Nevada Commission on Equal Rights of Citizens
New Hampshire Commission for Human Rights
New Hanover (N.C.) Human Relations Commission
New Haven, Connecticut, Commission on Equal Opportunities
New Jersey Division of Civil Rights, Department of Law and Public Safety
New Mexico Human Rights Commission
New York City (N.Y.) Commission on Human Rights
New York State Division on Human Rights
North Carolina State Office of Administrative Hearings
North Dakota Department of Labor
Ohio Civil Rights Commission
Oklahoma Human Rights Commission
Omaha (Nebr.) Human Relations Department
Oregon Bureau of Labor
Orlando (Fla.) Human Relations Department
Paducah, Kentucky, Human Rights Commission
Pennsylvania Human Relations Commission
Philadelphia (Pa.) Commission on Human Relations
Pinellas County, Florida, Affirmative Action Office
Pittsburgh (Pa.) Commission on Human Rights
Prince George's County (Md.) Human Relations Commission
Prince William County (Va.) Human Rights Commission
Rhode Island Commission for Human Rights
Richmond County (Ga.) Human Rights Commission
Rockville (Md.) Human Rights Commission
St. Louis (Mo.) Civil Rights Enforcement Agency
St. Paul (Minn.) Department of Human Rights
St. Petersburg (Fla.) Human Relations Division
Seattle (Wash.) Human Rights Commission
Sioux Falls (S.D.) Human Relations Commission
South Bend (Ind.) Human Rights Commission
South Carolina Human Affairs Commission
South Dakota Division of Human Rights

Springfield (Ohio) Human Relations Department
Tacoma (Wash.) Human Relations Commission
Tampa, Florida, Office of Community Relations
Tennessee Commission for Human Development
Texas Commission on Human Rights
Topeka, Kansas, Human Relations Commission
Utah Industrial Commission, Anti-Discrimination Division
Vermont Attorney General's Office, Civil Rights Division
Vermont Human Rights Commission
Virgin Islands Department of Labor
Virginia Council on Human Rights
Washington Human Rights Commission
West Virginia Human Rights Commission
Wheeling (W.Va.) Human Rights Commission
Wichita Falls, Texas, Human Relations Commission
Wisconsin Equal Rights Division, Department of Industry, Labor and Human
    Relations
Wisconsin State Personnel Commission
Wyoming Fair Employment Practices Commission
York (Pa.) Human Relations Commission
Youngstown (Ohio) Human Relations Commission

(b) The designated Notice Agencies are:

Arkansas Governor's Committee on Human Resources
Ohio Director of Industrial Relations
Raleigh (N.C.) Human Resources Department, Civil Rights Unit

APPENDIX 3

Selected Excerpts from Title VII

Sec 2000e-2 Unlawful employment practices

EMPLOYER PRACTICES

(a) It shall be an unlawful employment practice for an employer—

(1) to fail or refuse to hire or to discharge any individual, or otherwise to discriminate against any individual with respect to his compensation, terms, conditions, or privileges of employment, because of such individual's race, color, religion, sex, or national origin; or

(2) to limit, segregate, or classify his employees or applicants for employment in any way which would deprive or tend to deprive any individual of employment opportunities or otherwise adversely affect his status as an employee, because of such individual's race or color, religion, sex, or national origin.

EMPLOYMENT AGENCY PRACTICES

(b) It shall be an unlawful employment practice for an employment agency to fail or refuse to refer for employment, or otherwise to discriminate against, any individual because of his race, color, religion, sex, or national origin, or to classify or refer for employment any individual on the basis of his race, color, religion, sex, or national origin.

LABOR ORGANIZATION PRACTICES

(c) It shall be an unlawful employment practice for a labor organization—

(1) to exclude or to expel from its membership, or otherwise to discriminate against, any individual because of his race, color, religion, sex, or national origin;

(2) to limit, segregate, or classify its membership or applicants for membership, or to classify or fail or refuse to refer for employment any individual, in any way which would deprive or tend to deprive any individual of employment opportunities, or would limit such employment opportunities or otherwise adversely affect his status as an employee or as an applicant for employment, because of such individual's race, color, religion, sex, or national origin; or

(3) to cause or attempt to cause an employer to discriminate against an individual in violation of this section.

Sec 2000e-3 Other unlawful employment practices

(a) DISCRIMINATION FOR MAKING CHARGES, TESTIFYING, ASSISTING, OR PARTICIPATING IN ENFORCEMENT PROCEEDINGS

It shall be an unlawful employment practice for an employer to discriminate against any of his employees or applicants for employment, for an employment agency, or joint labor-management committee controlling apprenticeship or other training or retraining, including on-the-job training programs, to discriminate against any individual, or for a labor organization to discriminate against any member thereof or applicant for membership, because he has opposed any practice made an unlawful employment practice by this subchapter, or because he has made a charge, testified, assisted, or participated in any manner in an investigation, proceeding, or hearing under this subchapter.

Sec 2000e-4 Equal Employment Opportunity Commission

(a) CREATION; COMPOSITION; POLITICAL REPRESENTATION; APPOINTMENT; TERM; VACANCIES; CHAIRMAN AND VICE CHAIRMAN; DUTIES OF CHAIRMAN; APPOINTMENT OF PERSONNEL; COMPENSATION OF PERSONNEL

There is hereby created a Commission to be known as the Equal Employment Opportunity Commission, which shall be composed of five members, not more than three of whom shall be members of the same political party. Members of the Commission shall be appointed by the President by and with the advice and consent of the Senate for a term of five years. Any individual chosen to fill a vacancy shall be appointed only for the unexpired term of the member whom he shall succeed, and all members of the Commission shall continue to serve until their successors are appointed and qualified, except that no such member of the Commission shall continue to serve (1) for more than sixty days when the Congress is in session unless a nomination to fill such vacancy shall have been submitted to the Senate, or (2) after the adjournment *sine die* of the session of the Senate in which such nomination was submitted. The President shall designate one member to serve as Chairman of the Commission, and one member to serve as Vice Chairman. The Chairman shall be responsible on behalf of the Commission for the administrative operations of the Commission, and, except as provided in subsection (b) of this section, shall appoint, in accordance with the provisions of Title 5 governing appointments in the competitive service, such officers, agents, attorneys, administrative law judges, and employees as he deems necessary to assist it in the performance of its functions and to fix their compensation in accordance with the provisions of chapter 51 and subchapter III of chapter 53 of Title 5, relating to classification and General Schedule pay rates: *Provided,* That assignment, removal, and compensation of administrative law judges shall be in accordance with sections 3105, 3344, 5372, and 7521 of Title 5.

(g) POWERS OF COMMISSION

The Commission shall have power—

(1) to cooperate with and, with their consent, utilize regional, State, local, and other agencies, both public and private, and individuals;

(2) to pay to witnesses whose depositions are taken or who are summoned before the Commissions or any of its agents the same witness and mileage fees are as paid to witnesses in the courts of the United States;

(3) to furnish to persons subject to this subchapter such technical assistance as they may request to further their compliance with this subchapter or an order issued thereunder;

(4) upon request of (i) any employer, whose employees or some of them, or (ii) any labor organization, whose members or some of them, refuse or threaten to refuse to cooperate in effectuating the provisions of this subchapter, to assist in such effectuation by conciliation or such other remedial action as is provided by this subchapter;

(5) to make such technical studies as are appropriate to effectuate the purposes and policies of this subchapter and to make the results of such studies available to the public;

(6) to intervene in a civil action brought under section 2000e-5 of this title by an aggrieved party against a respondent other than a government, governmental agency or political subdivision.

Sec 2000e-5 Enforcement provisions

(b) Whenever a charge is filed by or on behalf of a person claiming to be aggrieved, or by a member of the Commission, . . . the Commission shall serve a notice of the charge (including the date, place and circumstances of the alleged unlawful employment practice) . . . and shall make an investigation thereof. Charges shall be in writing under oath or affirmation and shall contain such information and be in such form as the Commission requires. Charges shall not be made public by the Commission. If the Commission determines after such investigation that there is not reasonable cause to believe that the charge is true, it shall dismiss the charge and promptly notify the person claiming to be aggrieved and the respondent of its action. In determining whether reasonable cause exists, the Commission shall accord substantial weight to final findings and orders made by State or local authorities in proceedings commenced under State or local law pursuant to the requirements of subsections (c) and (d) of this section. If the Commission determines after such investigation that there is reasonable cause to believe that the charge is true, the Commission shall endeavor to eliminate any such alleged unlawful employment practice by informal methods of conference, conciliation, and persuasion. Nothing said or done during and as a part of such informal endeavors may be made public by the Commission, its officers or employees, or used as evidence in a subsequent proceeding without the written consent of the persons concerned. Any person who makes public information in violation of this subsection shall be fined not more than $1,000 or imprisoned for not more than one year, or both. The Commission shall make its determination on reasonable cause as promptly as possible and, so far as practicable, not later than one hundred and twenty days from the filing of the charge or, where applicable under subsection (c) or (d) of this section, from the date upon which the Commissions authorized to take action with respect to the charge.

(c) STATE OR LOCAL ENFORCEMENT PROCEEDINGS; NOTIFICATION OF STATE OR LOCAL AUTHORITY; TIME FOR FILING CHARGES WITH COMMISSION; COMMENCEMENT OF PROCEEDINGS

In the case of an alleged unlawful employment practice occurring in a State, or political subdivision of a State, which has a State or local law prohibiting the unlawful employment practice alleged and establishing or authorizing a State or local authority to grant or seek relief from such practice or to institute criminal proceedings with respect thereto upon receiving notice thereof, no charge may be filed under subsection (b) of this section by the person aggrieved before the expiration of sixty days after proceedings have been commenced under the State or local law, unless such proceedings have been earlier terminated, provided that such sixty-day period shall be extended to one hundred and twenty days during the first year after the effective date of such State or local law. If any requirement for the commencement of such proceedings is imposed by a State or local authority other than a requirement of the filing of a written and signed statement of the facts upon which the proceeding is based, the proceeding shall be deemed to have been commenced for the purposes of this subsection at the time such statement is sent by registered mail to the appropriate State or local authority.

(d) STATE OR LOCAL ENFORCEMENT PROCEEDINGS; NOTIFICATION OF STATE OR LOCAL AUTHORITY; TIME FOR ACTION ON CHARGES BY COMMISSION

In the case of any charge filed by a member of the Commission alleging an unlawful employment practice occurring in a State or political subdivision of a State which has a State or local law prohibiting the practice alleged and establishing or authorizing a State or local authority to grant or seek relief from such practice or to institute criminal proceedings with respect thereto upon receiving notice thereof, the Commission shall, before taking any action with respect to such charge, notify the appropriate State or local officials and, upon request, afford them a reasonable time, but not less than sixty days (provided that such sixty-day period shall be extended to one hundred and twenty days during the first year after the effective day of such State or local law), unless a shorter period is requested, to act under such State or local law to remedy the practice alleged.

(e) TIME FOR FILING CHARGES; TIME FOR SERVICE OF NOTICE OF CHARGE ON RESPONDENT; FILING OF CHARGE BY COMMISSION WITH STATE OR LOCAL AGENCY; SENIORITY SYSTEM

A charge under this section shall be filed within one hundred and eighty days after the alleged unlawful employment practice occurred and notice of the charge (including the date, place and circumstances of the alleged unlawful employment practice) shall be served upon the person against whom such charge is made within ten days thereafter, except that in a case of an unlawful employment practice with respect to which the person aggrieved has initially instituted proceedings with a State or local agency with authority to grant or seek relief from such practice or to institute criminal proceedings with respect thereto upon receiving notice thereof, such charge shall be filed by or on behalf of the person aggrieved within three hundred days after the alleged unlawful employment practice occurred, or within thirty days after receiving notice that the State or local agency has terminated the proceedings under the

State or local law, whichever is earlier, and a copy of such charge shall be filed by the Commission with the State or local agency.

(f)(1) If within thirty days after a charge is filed with the Commission or within thirty days after expiration of any period of reference under subsection (c) or (d) of this section, the Commission has been unable to secure from the respondent a conciliation agreement acceptable to the Commission, the Commission may bring a civil action against any respondent not a government, governmental agency, or political subdivision named in the charge. In the case of a respondent which is a government, governmental agency, or political subdivision, if the Commission has been unable to secure from the respondent a conciliation agreement acceptable to the Commission, the Commission shall take no further action and shall refer the case to the Attorney General who may bring a civil action against such respondent in the appropriate United States district court. The person or persons aggrieved shall have the right to intervene in a civil action brought by the Commission or the Attorney General in a case involving a government, governmental agency, or political subdivision. If a charge filed with the Commission pursuant to subsection (b) of this section is dismissed by the Commission, or if within one hundred and eighty days from the filing of such charge or the expiration of any period of reference under subsection (c) or (d) of this section, whichever is later, the Commission has not filed a civil action under this section or the Attorney General has not filed a civil action in a case involving a government, governmental agency, or political subdivision, or the Commission has not entered into a conciliation agreement to which the person aggrieved is a party, the Commission, or the Attorney General in a case involving a government, governmental agency, or political subdivision, shall so notify the person aggrieved and within ninety days after the giving of such notice a civil action may be brought against the respondent named in the charge (A) by the person claiming to be aggrieved or (B) if such charge was filed by a member of the Commission, by any person whom the charge alleges was aggrieved by the alleged unlawful employment practice. Upon application by the complainant and in such circumstances as the court may deem just, the court may appoint an attorney for such complainant and may authorize the commencement of the action without the payment of fees, costs, or security. Upon timely application, the court may, in its discretion, permit the Commission, or the Attorney General in a case involving a government, governmental agency, or political subdivision, to intervene in such civil action upon certification that the case is of general public importance. Upon request, the court may, in its discretion, stay further proceedings for not more than sixty days pending the termination of State or local proceedings described in subsection (c) or (d) of this section or further efforts of the Commission to obtain voluntary compliance.

(2) Whenever a charge is filed with the Commission and the Commission concludes on the basis of a preliminary investigation that prompt judicial action is necessary to carry out the purposes of this Act, the Commission, or

the Attorney General in a case involving a government, governmental agency, or political subdivision, may bring an action for appropriate temporary or preliminary relief pending final disposition of such charge. Any temporary restraining order or other order granting preliminary or temporary relief shall be issued in accordance with rule 65 of the Federal Rules of Civil Procedure. It shall be the duty of a court having jurisdiction over proceedings under this section to assign cases for hearing at the earliest practicable date and to cause such cases to be in every way expedited.

(g) If the court finds that the respondent has intentionally engaged in or is intentionally engaging in an unlawful employment practice charged in the complaint, the court may enjoin the respondent from engaging in such unlawful employment practice, and order such affirmative action as may be appropriate, which may include, but is not limited to, reinstatement or hiring of employees, with or without back pay (payable by the employer, employment agency, or labor organization, as the case may be, responsible for the unlawful employment practice), or any other equitable relief as the court deems appropriate. Back pay liability shall not accrue from a date more than two years prior to the filing of a charge with the Commission. Interim earnings or amounts earnable with reasonable diligence by the person or persons discriminated against shall operate to reduce the back pay otherwise allowable.

(k) In any action or proceeding under this subchapter the court, in its discretion, may allow the prevailing party, other than the Commission or the United States, a reasonable attorney's fee (including expert fees) as part of the costs, and the Commission and the United States shall be liable for costs the same as a private person.

Sec 2000e-7 Effect on State laws

Nothing in this subchapter shall be deemed to exempt or relieve any person from any liability, duty, penalty, or punishment provided by any present or future law of any State or political subdivision of a State, other than any such law which purports to require or permit the doing of any act which would be an unlawful employment practice under this subchapter.

Sec 2000e-8 Investigations

EXAMINATION AND COPYING OF EVIDENCE RELATED TO UNLAWFUL EMPLOYMENT PRACTICES

(a) In connection with any investigation of a charge filed under section 2000e-5 of this title, the Commission or its designated representative shall at all reasonable times have access to, for the purposes of examination, and the right to copy any evidence of any person being investigated or proceeded against that relates to unlawful employment practices covered by this subchapter and is relevant to the charge under investigation.

(e) It shall be unlawful for any officer or employee of the Commission to make public in any manner whatever any information obtained by the Commission pursuant to its authority under this section prior to the institution of any proceeding under this subchapter involving such information. Any officer or employee of the Commission who shall make public in any manner whatever any information in violation of this subsection shall be guilty of a misdemeanor and upon conviction thereof, shall be fined not more than $1,000 or imprisoned not more than one year.

Sec 2000-e12 Regulations . . .

(a) The Commission shall have authority from time to time to issue, amend, or rescind suitable procedural regulations to carry out the provisions of this subchapter. Regulations issued under this section shall be in conformity with the standards and limitations of subchapter II of chapter 5 of Title 5.

Index